A Necessary Grief

ESSENTIAL TOOLS FOR LEADERSHIP
IN BEREAVEMENT MINISTRY

A Necessary Grief

ESSENTIAL TOOLS FOR LEADERSHIP
IN BEREAVEMENT MINISTRY

LARRY J. MICHAEL

Printed in the United States of America

15 16 17 18 19 / 5 4 3 2 1

Dedicated to

KATHRYN
GOD'S GIFT OF GRACE AND LOVE

ALL GRIEVING PERSONS
WHOSE COURAGE INSPIRES

ALL LEADERS INVOLVED IN BEREAVEMENT MINISTRY
WHOSE COUNSEL AND CARE MAKE A HEALING DIFFERENCE

CONTENTS

ACKNOWLEDGMENTS

Writing a book is never a solo project because of the support and encouragement one receives from family, friends, and others who believe in the worth of the project.

I would like to acknowledge all of my family, with special recognition to the ones who were involved in different kinds of support along the way. Daughter Ashley provided some valued editing for which I am grateful. Ashley and Jason, Kent and Carmen, Graham and Sue, Allison and Kasey—were all great to encourage me; and the grandkids were a most welcome diversion—Walker, Esme, Luke, Abigail, Evelyn, Walt, Maxwell, Selah, Wyatt and baby (to be named soon) _____, and Michael on the way! Wife Kathryn was the epitome of loving encouragement and patience throughout—great are her rewards!

My Tuesday morning Men's Prayer Group must be given a "shout-out" as I inflicted a number of chapters on them, and their cajoling became a necessary prod to write—Bill, Bob, Byrd, Cody, Ed, Jeff, Larry, and remembering Dr. Dewey, who left us too soon.

A special thanks to grief authors Elizabeth Harper Neeld, Sherry Williams White, and Alan Wolfelt for their contribution to my understanding of grief and its application to bereavement ministry.

The staff, board, volunteers, and many members of the grief support groups I led while Executive Director of Alabama Grief Support Services all made a significant contribution to much that I have learned and continue to learn about the grieving process. Some have been mentioned, and some names have been changed to protect their privacy.

Grateful recognition to the editors and staff of Kregel Publications, who are most competent in their work and always ready to help. Dennis Hillman, the publisher, provided exceptional counsel along the way.

Lastly, thanks to my local church congregation, South Highland Presbyterian Church, who have provided Christian nurture and opportunities for ministry together, to the Lord God we all serve and love. Amen.

INTRODUCTION

*"… but one thing is necessary. Mary has made the right choice,
and it will not be taken away from her."*
Luke 10:42, HCSB

Only one thing is necessary. When Jesus visited the home of Mary and Martha, Mary sat at his feet while Jesus taught her. Martha was busy preparing the meal. She became irritated and told Jesus to tell Mary to help her. But Jesus reminded Martha that Mary had chosen the better thing.

In a world that runs away from grief, the better thing, the *one thing that is necessary*, is to face the grief, let grief be its own teacher, and recognize its importance in one's life. No one welcomes the struggles that accompany grief. But life is the richer and more meaningful for those who will do that which is necessary and work through their grief toward wholeness and healing.

This book was written for those who are involved in grief leadership, whether professionally or at the lay level. It is not a clinical work, but a practical work, intended to help leaders in three distinct ways. One: to give grief leaders a better handle on understanding grief and its impact on survivors. Two: to provide some practical tools for leaders to help those who are grieving. Three: to help leaders help others to reach out to those who are grieving.

A Necessary Grief has many ramifications for those who are willing to take those crucial steps needed to bring valuable ministry to those who have lost loved ones. I pray that it may be so.

PART I

COMPREHENDING GRIEF

CHAPTER ONE

DEFINING GRIEF AND MOURNING

Blessed are they that mourn: for they shall be comforted.
Matthew 5:4, KJV

People always seem to be running away from grief! Even at church. I stood at the display table that I had prepared. It was the occasion of a ministry fair at a local church, and I was invited as a guest vender, to share information about our grief agency. Many people rushed in between services to pay their respects to the local recipients of their outreach funds. While most of them migrated to the gift tables and mission trip tables, only a few meandered to my booth. Haltingly, they would walk up toward the table, cast a sideways glance to see who might be watching, and then venture to look more closely at the information. Perhaps a question would come about our work, but more often than not, I would have to engage them, and then usually, would discover that they themselves had suffered a loss that was still impacting their lives. A young boy about the age of ten came right up to the table, and started asking me questions about grief—what we do, who do we help, etc. It was so refreshing to see such interest from a child. But others reacted differently. One lady came as close as about five feet, then all of a sudden bolted from the room in tears. I only made slight eye contact with her, but she ran out before I could even speak. I later discovered that her mother died ten years ago. She was still grieving.

For the most part, we live in a world that runs away from grief as quickly as possible. Our culture seeks to avoid it, often acts like it doesn't exist, and seems to ignore the horrible effect grief can have on survivors. In fact, it has been speculated that perhaps many Americans today, with advances in longevity, consider that death may be optional. Certainly that is the way we seem to act as a society. But the reality is that one in three Americans experience the loss of a loved one every year. Nearly 1,000,000 people lose a spouse each year.[1] Around 300,000 children die every year.[2] There is plenty of grief to go around. And for leaders, one thing is necessary.

Pastors and Christian leaders are the ones who are called upon to minister to those individuals in our congregations and community who are grieving the loss of a loved one. That time in a person's life is crucial, and it is important for us to have a grasp of the nature of the grief that our parishioners are experiencing. Unfortunately, much of the training received in theological education does not deal with the practical issues that ministers face in reaching out to those who hurt among their congregation. Theological disciplines are essential to ministerial education, but some divinity schools and seminaries have grown lax in the more practical disciplines of pastoral care and counseling realms. Martha Grace Reese in her book *Unbinding the Gospel* lamented her theological training which did not prepare her to even lead a prayer in a difficult pastoral situation that she encountered early in her ministry[3]

> Nobody should have to die in pain. Nobody should have to die alone.
> —Ira Byock, *Dying Well.*

The temptation for many professionals is to fall back on what training they have received and do the best in the situations they face. While they offer some counsel and support, often they do not fully comprehend the depth of the emotional fallout that occurs in the lives of many grieving persons. So, what is important? Firstly, leaders should not separate themselves emotionally from the grief-stricken family. As a leader becomes a compassionate participant in the hurt, a relationship for sharing is established. It is necessary that leaders are in touch with their own feelings, and aware of the personal

1. http://usatoday30.usatoday.com/news/health/2010-08-11-widows11_ST_N.htm; accessed October 30, 2014.
2. http://www.theravive.com/research/The-Effects-of-the-Death-of-a-Child-on-a-Marriage; accessed October 30, 2014.
3. Martha Grace Reese, *Unbinding the Gospel* (St. Louis: Chalice Press, 2006), 61-62.

grief that they have experienced. Leaders are the individuals who will convey the love and grace and comfort of Christ to those persons who need them at this critical time. Demonstrating care and even showing emotion is part of that. In fact, the more leaders who can empathize and show that they are real people who can identify and connect at an experiential level with their parishioners, the greater will be the impact of their ministry to them.

Secondly, it is necessary to consider all the facets of grief and the multiple ways it impacts a person's life. In doing so, contrasting it with mourning will demonstrate the distinctions that will enable one to minister more effectively.

What Is Grief?

Grief may be defined briefly as the response to loss. More specifically, grief is the process of experiencing numerous physical, psychological, emotional, social, behavioral, and spiritual responses to some type of loss. Loss falls into two categories: psychosocial loss (death of a loved one, divorce, loss of purpose, etc.) and physical loss (health, job, home, possession, etc.). Both types represent loss that has brought change into our lives. For the most part, this book will deal with psychosocial loss, specifically death of a loved one.

DIFFERENT TYPES OF GRIEF

As has been stated, grief is not limited to death. People can have intense sorrowful reactions to any kind of loss. Some of the following are types of losses commonly experienced by those with whom we minister.

Nonfinite Grief

Nonfinite grief that occurs as a result of losing hopes, wishes, ideals, future expectations. We see nonfinite grief in families who have received the diagnosis of a chronic illness or developmental or neurological deficit in a family member. Families that have children diagnosed with autism, Down's Syndrome, hearing loss, seizure disorder, or other disabilities go through nonfinite grief. This grieving process is unique in that it is ongoing with loved ones who are physically present. When their child has an incident or set back, the grieving process is repeated. While other children are progressing through normal developmental phases at school, in sports, getting drivers' licenses, becoming married, etc., their child remains in a static condition with dependency on the parents and family. The family must seek creative ways for them to unite and become stronger with the challenges they face.

Wayne Atcheson, in his book *Our Family Was a Team,* shares how faith and mutual responsibility in his home while growing up helped his family deal lovingly with their oldest sibling "Junior" who suffered a severely debilitating brain injury at birth due to oxygen deprivation. Doctors said he wouldn't live to be more than eighteen, but because of the way the family rallied around Junior and lovingly functioned as a "team," and with the tender care of his mother, Junior lived to the age of forty-four. Junior never spoke one word his entire life, but he was a valued member of the Atcheson family from day one until his last breath on earth. Junior's early suffering was influential in the calling of Wayne's father to the ministry as a pastor, where he served faithfully for sixty-three years. Wayne and his brothers later rejoiced at the passing of their parents and their belief in the prospect that Junior then could speak fluently with his mama and daddy in heaven.

Ambiguous Loss

Ambiguous loss is another form of nonfinite grief that differs from normal loss because 1) there is no certainty of death, or 2) no certainty of the return to lucidity. The first example relates to when a person goes missing, is kidnapped, is lost at war, perished in a natural disaster (e.g., tsunami, hurricane, tornado, etc.), terrorist attack (e.g., 9/11 disaster, hijacked planes), or has simply disappeared from one's life. Most common in the latter would be abandonment, parental absence in divorce, or a child given up for adoption. There is no physical presence but there is a psychological presence. This type of ambiguous loss creates continuing consternation and anxiety about the loss of the person. There is little resolution, and the effects of grief may be relentless.

> With ambiguous loss there is no closure; the challenge is to learn how to live with the ambiguity.
> —Pauline Boss, Ph.D.

The second example of ambiguous loss is what persons experience when someone in their lives is present but not present, "still there" but also "not there." This type of loss occurs when a loved one has a cognitive impairment, suffering from dementia, a stroke, or some sort of traumatic injury to the brain. This is the type of loss most recognized when individuals who have dementia have days or moments of lucidity, when they are alert and their mind seems clear. Disappointment and frustration arises when they return to their state of confusion, and renewed grief occurs. One can feel anger as well, not understanding the process of the illness and their inability to maintain their clarity.[4]

Anticipatory Grief

Anticipatory grief describes the process of grieving, adapting, and coping that commences before (in anticipation of) the loss, such as the initiation of divorce proceedings or when a loved one is diagnosed with a terminal illness. A pastor is called upon to provide comfort and support when parishioners are dealing with anticipatory grief. As a pastor, there were many times that I found myself at the bedside of individuals facing their pending death. On one occasion, I had visited the hospital to see a member named Ben who had been struggling with cancer for some time. On this occasion, I arrived in the room just as he was due to be released to go home. His wife and daughter were there and were encouraged that he was about to be discharged. He had changed into his street clothes and was putting on his shoes. Then something unexpected happened. He experienced an acute physical reaction that brought the nurses running into the room.

In just a short while, Ben began to have a dramatic reversal, and the complications related to his cancer became life-threatening. The situation grew increasingly worse, and in just a few hours the whole family had been called in to his bedside. Instead of taking him home, they were forced to deal with the prospect of his imminent death. I remained with the family and maintained a night-long vigil with them, not always knowing how I could best help. Certainly my presence was appreciated, and I offered prayers and Scripture reading at the request of the family. Occasionally, I took a cold cloth and wiped Ben's perspiring brow in an effort to provide some physical relief. After a grueling night of wrestling with the inevitable, Ben died shortly before dawn, with the blessing and release of his family into the arms of God. At that point the anticipatory

---

4. For more information on ambiguous loss and easing its effects, see Pauline Boss, *Loss, Trauma, and Resilience: Therapeutic Work with Ambiguous Loss* (New York: W. W. Norton & Company, 2006).

grief became real loss of physical life with all the ramifications of normal grief. We joined hands and hearts around his bed, thanked God for Ben's life, and commended him to the Lord's keeping.

On another occasion, a couple came into my office shortly after receiving bad news from the doctors. The wife was told that she had been diagnosed with Alzheimer's disease. She was relatively young, and the devastation of that news was a horrible pronouncement for their life plans. I counseled and prayed with them, but not long after that, her condition deteriorated to the point that she had to be taken to a nursing facility where she remained until her death a few years later. Life has many twists and turns, and the many forms of grief can take their toll on individuals and families.

With anticipatory grief the leader plays an important role in helping people to understand some of the things that they are feeling and experiencing. While leaders may not know how they feel exactly, they are in a position to give guidance to grief survivors about issues they undoubtedly will face. Elizabeth Kübler-Ross's *On Death and Dying*, a classic work on anticipatory grief, is a great primer for helping individuals face pending death. Another helpful book is *Saying Goodbye: How Families Can Find Renewal through Loss*, by Dr. Joseph Nowinski and Dr. Barbara Okun. This book helps families communicate with their loved ones regarding plans and preparation while facing terminal illness.

The partnership of hospice care with ministry is extremely effective in helping families prepare for their loved one's passing. Lovingly, hospice nurses and chaplains are there to help bring guidance in the process of separation and giving permission for the loved one to go. Interestingly enough, I have been told by hospice nurses that people of faith seem to survive longer than some who do not express such faith. The hospice personnel say that

> Anticipatory grief, I believe, is a myth—there is no such thing. When we maintain hope, we never accept or prepare for death when it strikes. We cannot anticipate the pain of separation, no matter how it happens. Sudden death and long-term illness are two side roads that merge into the same main road of survival—to accept the unacceptable.
> —Mitch Carmody, *Living with Loss Magazine,* Fall 2010

this is so because these individuals have such a strong will to live, and their appreciation of life's merits is so valued. With proper expression, loved ones are eased through the transition from this life to the next.

The minister or leader is presented with a unique opportunity to explore a person's relationship of faith in his or her final days. Preparation for eternity is a matter of significance for those who believe in an afterlife. I have noted over the years there have been many times individuals wanted to make their peace with God when they sensed the end was near. Quite a few have responded in faith to a loving God, even in the twilight hours of their lives. It is a beautiful thing to behold the tranquility that comes when the resolution of faith becomes a reality.

Still, the shock is great when a loved one dies, regardless of how much preparation has been made for the inevitable. Mitch Carmody, a grief author, lost his son who had succumbed to a bout with cancer. Mitch accepted the fact that his son was going to die, but the father later realized that he was still not prepared for his son's death. He came to believe that there is no such thing as anticipatory grief.[5] That debate may be left for the experts. All that a leader can do during times of anticipation is to be present throughout the process with a family, ministering through care and grace.

One helpful measure is to counsel the family and individual concerned to have an Advance Medical Directive that includes a living will, power of attorney, and health care proxy. The purpose of this document is to convey the person's wishes and preferences in regard to medical treatments and interventions.[6] In addition, the involvement of a hospice service is a great help in the final days of a person's life. In my experience, the nurses and chaplains have been sensitive, caring, and have offered great counsel to families dealing with the pending death of a loved one.

Normal Grief

Normal grief could be described as the typical reactions that people experience when they receive the news that a loved one has died. While

5. Mitch Carmody, "An Epiphany in Old San Juan," www.opentohope.com/an-epiphany-in-old-san-juan/; accessed October 30, 2014. Mitch Carmody wrote a book titled *Letters to My Son: A Journey through Grief* (Edina, MN: Beaver's Pond Press, 2002).

6. See www.medicinenet.com/advance_medical_directives/article.htm; for more information and counsel on advance medical directives; accessed October 30, 2014.

we may see the normality of their grief, most grievers think that nothing is normal. It becomes a time of emotional volatility, uncharacteristic behavior, and sometimes irrational thoughts. One of the most appreciated sessions we use in our grief groups is "So, You Think You're Going Crazy."[7] Grievers identify with that overwhelming feeling that they have when their world is turned upside down. Nothing seems normal, and they feel like they may be losing their minds. But they're not. They are grieving.

Normal physical reactions are unusual aggressiveness, sleep abnormality, loss of appetite, crying, and susceptibility to illness. Emotional responses of shock, fear, sadness, numbness, anger, loneliness, and hopelessness frequently occur. Mental confusion, forgetfulness, being in a daze, and lack of concentration, all accompany normal grief experiences. More attention will be given to these responses in chapter two. The difference between normal grief and abnormal grief is that all of these responses are situational and with proper attention will ease in time. Abnormal grief may take the long term form of reclusiveness, chronic depression, suicidal tendencies, and loss of the will to live.

When a person's loved one dies, nothing seems normal. And that in itself is normal. So, be patient with those who are grieving. The person's life has changed, and compassionate understanding is the best response a leader can offer.

Traumatic Grief

Grief may be particularly traumatic following a sudden, unexpected death when a person's normal coping mechanisms are overtaxed by the tragedy. As a young boy, I recall going with my father (who was a pastor) to the home of a family whose husband/father was killed in a tragic accident on a construction site. The man was operating a large wheel loader on an earthmoving job. Somehow, the loader got out of control, the brakes failed, and it was unstoppable as a runaway machine accelerating down a steep mountain. The only thing he could do to save himself was to jump off the racing loader, but unfortunately he fell the wrong way and the machine crushed him in its path. The family was utterly shattered—distraught and devastated by the news. I watched and observed as my father brought his own unique brand of comfort to a desperate situation. He prayed a beautiful

---

7. Based on an article by Dr. Alan Wolfelt, *Centering Cooperation and Grief Digest Magazine.*

prayer, held them all close, and offered spiritual counsel in answering their questions about eternal life, and how they must cope in the days ahead. More significantly, he was there for them for a long time afterward.

Complicated Grief

Complicated grief occurs when grief becomes chronic, disabling, and more intense. This is often seen as a progression of grief into major depression, with some features of post-traumatic stress disorder, such as nightmares and flashbacks. Complicated grief is not recognized by the American Psychiatric Association.[8] According- ing to a study reported in the *Journal of the American Medical Association*, about ten to twenty percent of people grieving the loss of a loved one ex- perience complicated grief.[9] One example was a widow who came to one of our support groups, after becoming a recluse in her bedroom for over three years. She finally realized that she was not any better, and the pain of being stuck in her grief was overwhelming. She reached out for help, heard about our support group, and struck up the courage to attend. It was an important step for her to take.

> ### Along the Road
>
> I walked a mile with pleasure
> She chattered all the way,
> But left me none the wiser
> For all she had to say.
>
> I walked a mile with sorrow
> And ne'er a word said she;
> But oh, the things I learned from her
> When sorrow walked with me.
> —Robert Browning Hamilton

When a tornado ripped through Alabama and much of the South in April 2011, there was much trauma and grief after 243 individuals lost their lives. Communities came together and rallied around the survivors. First responder teams came in and helped deal with the task of trying to

---

8. Cited at www.health.harvard.edu/fhg/updates/Complicated-grief.shtml; accessed October 30, 2014. "Complicated grief is not one of the disorders in the American Psychiatric Association official diagnostic manual."

9. Shear, K. et al. "Treatment of Complicated Grief: A Randomized Controlled Trial," *Journal of the American Medical Association* (June 1, 2005): Vol. 293, No. 21, 2601–8.

normalize the situation and bring immediate relief, shelter, and medical attention. But, the grief would come later. I had one elderly man in a grief support group who had lost his wife of sixty-four years in December. When the tornado came through in April, he lost his granddaughter and her two children, who had unfortunately sought shelter in a friend's garage. He lamented that he was covered up with grief. As a result of the tornado tragedy, complications arose as families not only dealt with their immediate loss of home and possessions, but the long-term loss of their loved ones who would not return. Churches, but also ministers, neighbors, mission groups, athletic teams, and relief disaster teams, brought loving care and attention that continued in the communities for an extended period of time.

THE DIFFERENCE BETWEEN GRIEF AND MOURNING

Grief and mourning are often used interchangeably by many people. They both seem to represent the same experience, but in fact they are very different. Stated simply, one experience is inward, the other is outward. Grief is the inward process that involves our thoughts and feelings after experiencing loss. Mourning is the outward process that involves the expression of our grief. It is often referred to as "grief that has gone public." (Not to confuse the issue, but bereavement is another word associated with grief. Bereavement is the state of being in grief).

> Some day you're gonna look back on this moment of your life as such a sweet time of grieving. You'll see that you were in mourning and your heart was broken, but your life was changing....
> —*Elizabeth Gilbert*

Why is it so important to know the difference between grief and mourning? Since grief is an inward process, it can sometimes be masked by appearances and occur unnoticed by others around the person. You can grieve inwardly while your heart is being torn apart, experience bewilderment in your loss, and yet not express it in an outward capacity. When persons mourn, they find ways to vent their grief, to get it out. It may mean tears and crying, retelling the story of your loved one's death, visiting the cemetery, planting a tree, hanging a wreath, wearing black, holding a special memorial service on occasion, and so on.

The problem is, that when it comes to mourning, society is not very patient with long-term expression of grief. Often there are comments like, "Isn't it time you got over your husband's death?" "Don't you think you need to move on with your life?" These are a few examples of the insensitivity that people can demonstrate in their lack of understanding with regard to the nature and length of time that is involved in the grief process. Actually, it may be more about the awkwardness they feel themselves, rather than their concern for the person's recovery.

There are examples of mourning in the Bible. One prominent example is illustrated in the life of King David of Israel. When he lost his son Absalom, who had been rebellious and attempted to overthrow his father, David lamented his son's untimely death. David loved Absalom, and his expression of mourning is memorable—*"The king was shaken. He went up to the room over the gateway and wept. As he went, he said: "O my son Absalom! My son, my son Absalom! If only I had died instead of you—O Absalom, my son, my son!"* (2 Sam. 18:33, NIV). These are the words of a father, a parent in deep distress and overwhelming grief. The anguish and pain were so intense that those around him could not comprehend it. David's son had turned against him and David's army had been victorious in battle. In effect, David had taken the very life of his son to preserve his throne. But the victory paled in significance to the loss of his son. It was like losing part of himself. The aching void of a tragic life that had been lost with all hopes for reconciliation and restoration between father and son were dashed to the grave. It was a grief of regret, remorse, and bitterness. Only a father who loved his son regardless of the circumstances could understand.

> He who has no time to mourn, has no time to mend.
> —John Donne

THE DISTINCTION OF EACH PERSON'S GRIEF

Every person's grief experience is unique and different from anyone else. There are many factors that affect that distinction, and it is important for leaders to be aware of them when ministering to a person who is grieving. Dr. Wayne Oates, in his classic book *Your Particular Grief*, lists five things that determine one's "particular" experience in grief—the person's unique relationship with the deceased; the circumstances of the death; previous experience with grief; the timeliness or untimeliness of the death; and the spiritual resources of the mourner. To these factors I would add "personal characteristics."

The Unique Relationship

The person who is grieving had a relationship with that person that was different from any other person. Whether it was a spouse, a child, a parent, a sibling, or a best friend—they had a certain type of relationship. The quality of the relationship with the deceased directly relates to the nature and depth of the grief. It appears most often that the stronger the relationship, the greater the loss. Individuals who have lost spouses say that they have lost half of themselves. It has been called "an emotional earthquake."

And then, there are those who had difficult relationships with the deceased. They grieve not only what the relationship was, but what it might have been. One man told me he grieved more over his mother, with whom his relationship was strained, than over his father with whom he had been very close throughout his lifetime. He was more settled and at peace with his father's passing, but still felt great angst over unresolved issues with his mother.

The Manner of Death or Loss

The circumstances surrounding the death have a great deal of impact on the surviving loved one. If the death is sudden as with a heart attack or stroke, there is great shock. Car accidents, plane crashes, violent acts, all so unexpected, create such an overwhelming response of disbelief. Once I conducted the funeral of a young man who had been stabbed to death. The trauma that accompanied the death contributed to the pallor over the whole service. The family were in such a state of shock and numb with their grief. How different it was to those occasions when a person died after a long lingering illness. In some measure, it provided the opportunity for loved ones to prepare for the death. But it still is a shock when it happens. Do not underestimate the significance of the manner of death. It impacts loved ones greatly, and they often tell and retell the story of how their loved one died. Show patience and care to them.

Previous Experience with Grief

Those persons who have experienced grief before will meet a new grief in a different manner than someone who has not. Their prior experience informs them regarding what to expect, even though each grief experience is unique to itself. If they have experienced other previous losses, they will reflect on the manner in which they dealt with them and how their lives were affected. Stirred remembrances will bring forth emotions that will rear their ugly heads as persons relive previous grief experiences when a new loss occurs. One lady that I knew lost her husband at a young age through a heart attack. Little did she know at the time that her young son would die some years later as a young man in the same way as her husband did. Her grief was doubled as she relived the grief she had experienced with her husband that was tragically repeated with her son.

Other previous losses related to job, divorce, or broken relationships will also impact a person's capacity to mourn the loss of a loved one. They may appear distracted or detached—characteristics that may be attributed to other things that have impacted their lives.

The Timeliness or Untimeliness of the Loss

People die at different ages, from infants in cribs to senior adults residing in nursing home facilities. When children die, it seems so unfair. To parents, it is out of sync that their child would die before them. It isn't right. When someone lives a long life, then it's expected that the time will come for them to depart. But it is still difficult to let them go. When someone is struck down in middle age, still full of hope and plans for the future, it also seems untimely. Perhaps we think that a timely death relates to someone else. But, when it comes home to roost, it is hard to accept timing regardless.

The Spiritual Resources of the Mourner

People of faith have a great resource to help them manage their grief journey. The belief in eternal life and knowing their loved one was a person of faith brings unbelievable comfort and hope. I remember leading a funeral in England many years ago, and the family gave no evidence of faith in their lives. When we came to the graveside, the wailing mother tried to throw herself in the grave of her young daughter. The family expressed no real belief in eternal life, and it was evident throughout the service and committal. I grieved for them in their hopelessness. How different that experience was in comparison to the numerous times I have been at the grave of loved ones who expressed their faith in the real hope they had of eternal life, and seeing their loved one again in the age to come.

Personal Characteristics

There are distinctive characteristics about the person who is grieving that will affect their dealing with grief and loss. One cannot overlook personality—whether a person is an extravert or introvert, expresses feelings or is more private, faces issues or runs from them. Many factors, even a person's health, can impact how they grieve. Some grief experts have pointed out the gender differences and how they can also impact grief, with men often being more inward in their grief and women being more expressive in their mourning. Generalities don't always apply, but certain tendencies can be noted.

It is critical to know the difference between grief and mourning. Both processes are there to help the bereaved face the reality that their loved one is gone and then to slowly begin to accommodate to that fact. A leader can play a crucial role in helping the bereaved navigate these waters that they have not encountered before. Being there for them is the most important aspect. Offering gentle guidance, praying with them, and supporting them will make a huge difference in encouraging the healing that needs to occur in their lives.

THE MOURNER'S BILL OF RIGHTS

Clergy and other leaders must help people to know the need for mourning and to give expression to it, regardless of how others may respond around them. Alan Wolfelt, noted grief author and Director of the Center for Loss and Life Transition in Fort Collins, Colorado, has written about the Mourner's Bill of Rights—ten specific ways for grievers to ascertain the difference between helpful and hurtful responses.[10]

---

10. Used by permission, Dr. Alan Wolfelt, www.centerforloss.com.

1. **You have the right to experience your own unique grief.**

    No one else will grieve in exactly the same way you do. So, when you turn to others for help, don't allow them to tell what you should or should not be feeling.

2. **You have the right to talk about your grief.**

    Talking about your grief will help you heal. Seek out others who will allow you to talk as much as you want, as often as you want, about your grief. If at times you don't feel like talking, you also have the right to be silent.

3. **You have the right to feel a multitude of emotions.**

    Confusion, disorientation, fear, guilt, and relief are just a few of the emotions you might feel as part of your grief journey. Others may try to tell you that feeling angry, for example, is wrong. Don't take these judgmental responses to heart. Instead, find listeners who will accept your feelings without condition.

4. **You have the right to be tolerant of your physical and emotional limits.**

    Your feelings of loss and sadness will probably leave you feeling fatigued. Respect what your body and mind are telling you. Get daily rest. Eat balanced meals. And don't allow others to push you into doing things you don't feel ready to do.

5. **You have the right to experience "grief bursts."**

    Sometimes, out of nowhere, a powerful surge of grief may overcome you. This can be frightening, but is normal and natural. Find someone who understands and will let you talk it out.

6. You have the right to make use of ritual.

The funeral ritual does more than acknowledge the death of someone loved. It helps provide you with the support of caring people. More importantly, the funeral is a way for you to mourn. If others tell you the funeral or other healing rituals such as these are silly or unnecessary, don't listen.

7. You have the right to embrace your spirituality.

If faith is a part of your life, express it in ways that seem appropriate to you. Allow yourself to be around people who understand and support your religious beliefs. If you feel angry at God, find someone to talk with who won't be critical of your feelings of hurt and abandonment.

8. You have the right to search for meaning.

You may find yourself asking, "Why did he or she die? Why this way? Why now?" Some of your questions may have answers, but some may not. And watch out for the clichéd responses some people may give you. Comments like, "It was God's will," or "Think of what you have to be thankful for" are not helpful and you do not have to accept them.

9. You have the right to treasure your memories.

Memories are one of the best legacies that exist after the death of someone loved. You will always remember. Instead of ignoring your memories, find others with whom you can share them.

10. You have the right to move toward your grief and heal.

Reconciling your grief will not happen quickly. Remember, grief is a process, not an event. Be patient and tolerant with yourself and avoid people who are impatient and intolerant with you. Neither you nor those around you must forget that the death of someone loved changes your life forever.

CONCLUSION

Dr. Wolfelt has beautifully summarized the needs that mourners have to give expression to their grief through mourning. People surrounding grievers will allow them to grieve inwardly with no limits. They may not be as tolerant, however, when it comes to public expressions of mourning. This evident impatience with grievers comes in many different ways, but can come in veiled comments like, "Are you feeling better yet?" What they usually mean is "I think you should be over this by now," or "It's time to get on with your life." People will put subtle pressure on grievers to be their old selves again. But the old self is now a thing of the past, and a new beginning with appropriate counsel is what the griever needs.

Leaders should not succumb to the temptation to "fix" people. Shakespeare wrote that "Every one can master a grief but he that has it." The grief process is a long one, and requires patience by those who support the survivors. Those who grieve inwardly also have a right to express their mourning in a public manner as long as is necessary for their healing.

Grieving and mourning are as natural as eating and breathing. Avoiding them to circumvent the pain complicates healing and delays opportunities to enjoy life once again. Knowing more about how grief manifests itself, and how to give expression to mourning, are positive ways for grievers to deal with their loss. Leaders are there to offer comfort, solace, and guidance in ways that will facilitate healing and wholeness, as dictated by the need of each situation.

CHAPTER TWO

HOW GRIEF IMPACTS INDIVIDUALS

"We do not want you to ... grieve as others do who have no hope."
1 Thessalonians 4:13, ESV

I met Ginger at the educational seminar for grief leaders. She had been widowed for six years, but revealed that she was still grieving the loss of her husband. As well, she had suffered numerous physical symptoms for some time related to her grief. Among those symptoms was chronic chest pain. All kinds of medical diagnostic tests had been conducted the last several years, yet there was never a conclusive determination of any real physical problem. At the conference, the leader asked her about her husband's death. She replied that he had died in a tragic accident. They owned a farm outside of town, and he drove his truck out to the farm to attend to some business there. When he got to the farm, there was a gate which had to be opened. So, he stopped the truck which was on an incline, and got out to unlock the gate. He had unfortunately left the truck running. The brake failed and the truck ran over him, killing him instantly. Ginger shared that his chest had been crushed. The leader mentioned that often there is transference from someone who has died, that the surviving relative often experiences pain associated with the death. At that moment, Ginger realized that she had been suffering chest pain as part of the grief related to her husband's death. It was a revolutionary discovery for her, and gave her much relief to realize how grief had affected her life, including physical manifestations.

Grief impacts the whole person. This means that there is no area of a grieving person's life that remains untouched. An individual may not experience everything that will be discussed in this chapter. Much of what people experience depends on the intensification of grief. As a leader, it is necessary to become aware of the many faces of grief in a person's life and how one may best be of help during those times. Awareness of the physical, emotional, cognitive, social, and spiritual responses to grief will enable a leader to become more responsive to what may be happening in the griever's particular situation.

PHYSICAL

Grief can be so overwhelming that the full impact of it can actually kill a person. I traveled to Scotland recently. And while there, I visited Edinburgh Castle. At the top of the castle sits the oldest building in the country, a tiny little chapel dedicated to St. Margaret. Margaret was the queen of Scotland, married to King Malcolm III, a man who was uncouth and illiterate, but his wife did her best to improve his social skills. Malcolm held great admiration for his wife. She was a very pious woman, deeply devoted to her faith, and was engaged in many acts of charity. She reached out to orphans and the poor, committing herself to these tasks each day before she ate any food. She rose at midnight every night to attend worship services. Her piety was greatly acclaimed in the land. But she was not above the impact of loss. In 1093 her husband and their oldest son

> Happiness has gone out of our lives;
> Grief has taken the place of our dances.
> —Lamentations 5:15, GNT

Edward went off to fight against the English. Shortly thereafter, Margaret received the terrible news that they had both been killed in battle. Her grief was so great that she succumbed and died in three days. Not yet fifty years of age, her death was attributed to a broken heart.

Granted that this case is undoubtedly an exception generally speaking, the ramifications of grief can take a tremendous physical toll on a person. In most cases, numbness, shock and denial enable a person to cope with the immediate impact of the news. These are tremendous ways in which God has equipped persons to respond in the early stages of grief. Otherwise, the shock could prove devastating. But the physical toll can still be great. As part of the individual's way of handling the stress and anxiety of his or her loss experience, the following are possible physical sensations/reactions that are considered to be a normal component of grief:

Changes in appetite:

- Indulging in food; binge eating
- Lack of eating; loss of appetite; upset stomach

Sleep disturbances:

- Oversleeping; difficulty falling asleep; inability to get started/motivated for another day
- Sleep deprivation; nightmares; dreaming about their loved ones; multiple awakenings

Exaggeration of other physical situations:

- Blood pressure; diabetes; allergies; headaches/migraines; trouble with breathing; oversensitivity to noise
- Clenched jaws; tight feelings in the throat and chest; neck or back pain; tenseness; dizziness; trembling; dry mouth; exhaustion; muscular weakness; lack of energy

While this is not an exhaustive list, it gives an indication of the physical deficiencies that can accompany one's grief. As a complication, these physical impairments may make a person relatively vulnerable to more acute and severe illnesses. The role of a leader is not to try to play doctor, but to encourage persons to seek appropriate help for their situation. They may not always recognize what is happening to them, and counsel about the ways grief can impact a person may prove beneficial. It will definitely help them "normalize" their grief, and not feel that their symptoms are unusual or weird.

People are often driven to seek immediate solutions to their physical problems. Sometimes this can lead to a dependence on substances like prescription drugs or alcohol, which can lead to devastating consequences. I knew one person whose family were called upon to intervene because of her drug addiction after she had experienced a significant loss. She was convinced in her mind that she was only doing what the doctor told her to do. But it had gone way beyond any positive affects to a disposition and state that affected her and all the people around her. When the intervention occurred, she was very angry and believed everyone was against her, including me as her pastor. But she needed help. She was admitted to a treatment center, and her response to the program proved successful long term.

Certain treatments may be helpful in the short term, but the person still must inevitably face reality and the issues related to grief. The physical symptoms that can come with grief will recede in time as a person works through issues and receives appropriate support. But at times the physical reactions may seem unbearable. Counsel and comfort they receive will go a long way in helping them move forward. But, if physical difficulties persist and symptoms increase, it is wise for individuals to be advised to contact their physician.

When a person begins to adjust to the loss, the physical symptoms lessen. Such positive changes as heightened energy levels, stable sleeping patterns, a stronger immune system, and a sense of physical well-being will occur. Engaging in some form of physical exercise each day is a great way of improving physical health during the grief process. While the physical exertion is good for the body, it is also great for the mind. Even a half-hour of walking can help to improve stamina and enhance one's physical condition.

EMOTIONAL

Florida is known as the "Sunshine State." I lived there for some time, serving as a pastor, and enjoyed the climate and the people. I had the great privilege of knowing a young minister named Mark Stephens, who had served as the interim pastor of our church before my calling there. He had a beautiful wife and three daughters, served as an extension director of one of our seminaries, and was brilliant, compassionate, and gifted in so many ways. He embarked on a strict regimen of dieting and cycling that enabled him to lose a lot of weight and get in the greatest shape of his life, or so he thought. Mark was especially excited about his cycling, and the opportunities he might have in making friendships and sharing his faith when appropriate.

One particular Sunday changed things forever. It was a typical day in many ways—he had preached that morning in a local church, enjoyed having lunch with his family, cycled in the afternoon, and decided to relax and watch some TV that evening. Then later that night my phone rang. I had just gone to bed. It was Mark's wife. She told me that they had just gotten back from the hospital. And then she said, "Mark just died." I was shocked and dumbfounded. I told her I would come over to their house right away. I quickly dressed, and arrived about the same time as two other pastors from our church. Of course, she and the girls were overwhelmed, emotional, and distraught. Mark's parents, who lived some distance away, arrived a short while later. They were all in shock and total disbelief, as the rest of us were.

I and the other pastors were caught up in the emotional turmoil of this dear family. We were all grasping for words of comfort and consolation. Mark was so young. It just seemed incomprehensible. We learned that Mark had suffered a fatal heart attack. He did not realize that he had heart disease. I and the other pastors did our best to bring some sense of solace to this shocking situation. My heart was wrenching for this dear family who were experiencing every emotion that one would feel in such devastating circumstances. His mother pleaded for us to join together, to pray and seek God's comfort and understanding—how much we all needed it. And so we did, expressing our love for Mark and pleading for God to embrace this dear family in this hour of need. But the overwhelming sense of sadness and disbelief affected us all. Every imaginable emotion was in that room. We were all Christians. We rejoiced that Mark was with the Lord, but we were utterly numbed and heartsick at Mark's sudden departure.

The whole spectrum of emotions that were felt that night at Mark's home are indicative of the many ways that emotions can grip persons who are grieving. These are some of the most common emotions:

- Shock and disbelief—At the time of impact, right after a loved one has died, it can be hard to accept what happened. The griever may feel numb and have trouble believing that the loss really happened, evading the reality of death. "I just can't believe this has happened." "I feel like this is all a bad dream." These are typical statements made by someone experiencing shock.

- Denial—shortly after the initial shock, people will experience a period when they refuse to acknowledge that the person is gone. They distract themselves thoroughly so that they won't have to think about the loss. One lady said that her husband always traveled and she just imagined he was on a trip. But several weeks later, she realized this time he wasn't coming back. Alan Wolfelt uses the term "evasion," which is more positive than denial, and alludes to the way that averting the reality of the death can aid a person in traversing the early days of grief.

- Sadness—Profound sadness is probably one of the most universally experienced symptoms of grief. Grieving individuals may have feelings of emptiness, despair, yearning, or deep loneliness. They may also cry a lot or feel emotionally unstable. The idea is prominent in our culture that tears are a sign of weakness and lack of strength. But, the release that occurs with emotions is healing and cathartic. Studies reveal that tears contain certain toxic chemicals released by the response to stress. When these tensions are released, they help a person to begin to heal. Stress creates certain chemical imbalances in the body, and some researchers believe that tears remove toxic substances and help re-establish homeostasis. These tears are somewhat different in make-up than tears that come from eye irritation. Mood-altering chemicals like catecholamine is present in tears of emotion.[1] So, there is great benefit from tears that are shed by grievers.

- Guilt—Grievers may have strong feelings of regret or feel guilty about things they did or did not say or do. It's what we call the "shoulda coulda woulda" syndrome. The "if onlys" will become an obsession if not dealt with. "Why didn't I...? "What if this

> Guilt is perhaps the most painful companion to death.
> —Elisabeth Kübler-Ross

---

1. William J. Worden, *Grief Counseling and Grief Therapy: A Handbook for the Mental Health Practitioner* (New York: Springer Publ. Co., 4th ed., 2009).

hadn't...?" "How could I have not realized...?" Persons will beat themselves up repeatedly, and need someone who will help them comprehend better the reality of the situation and deal with unnecessary guilt.

- Anger—Even if the loss was nobody's fault, grievers may feel angry and resentful. They may feel the need to blame someone for the injustice that was done to them. Their anger may turn toward God or other people who appear happy around them, or they become angry at the loved one for leaving them. One lady said she has gone to her husband's grave and kicked the dirt because she was angry that he left her.

- Fear—A significant loss can trigger a host of worries and fears. Grievers may feel anxious, helpless, or insecure. They may even have panic attacks; fears of getting through each day; of being alone; of managing as a single parent. They ask, "What will I do now?"

Facing the death of a loved one often makes people reflect on their own mortality. They may begin to worry about their own death, or who will take care of those they leave behind, especially little children. Thinking about one's own death can be a scary prospect. If their loved one died after a long illness, they may worry that they could get the same disease. Then there's fear of the unknown. How will they go on, and what lies ahead for them?

> No one ever told me that grief felt so like fear. I am not afraid, but the sensation is like being afraid. The same fluttering in the stomach, the same restlessness, the yawning. I keep on swallowing.
> —C.S. Lewis, *A Grief Observed*

- Hopelessness—There may be the feeling that life is not worth living any more, that they cannot go on without their loved one. There may be a desire to just give up, to become listless, and a recluse. Christian leaders have an opportunity to point grievers toward the hope that is steadfast and sure, the hope of eternal life through Jesus Christ. The apostle Paul wrote: "We do not want you to … grieve as others do who have no hope" (1 Thess. 4:13, ESV).

- Stress—Many of us think about Post-Traumatic Stress Disorder (PTSD) in relation to soldiers returning from war or living through natural disasters. But the death of a loved one may also be a traumatic event in a person's life. If one witnessed the death, or were present during an illness or accident, he or she can suffer from PTSD, experiencing painful flashbacks, sleep problems, or other symptoms.

- Anxiety—There may arise an anxiety that results from all the combined emotions listed. This takes stress to another level, and may be more significant as a contributing factor toward complicated grief.

The task of the leader is to help grieving individuals experience and express appropriately all the emotions that they may feel. Give them permission to own their feelings. They should not be judged, but accepted as they are, and allowed to give voice to all that has happened. Leaders represent an emotional constant because of the strength that is represented to them. Grievers should be offered comfort, consolation, and empathy. A little compassion and tenderness

> To weep is to make less the debt of grief.
> —*William Shakespeare*

go a long way in enabling persons to know that their leader really cares about them and how they feel. These times often serve to bring leaders and people together, because of shared experiences, and the fact that their leaders were there for them at the time they needed them most.

COGNITIVE

"What was I thinking?" Bob asked himself as he was driving down the highway to a destination unknown. Bob had lost his wife recently and seemed to be in a regular state of confusion. Now he was in the car, and he knew he needed to go somewhere. But he couldn't remember where he was supposed to be going. He was in a fog but he kept driving, and then finally it dawned on him: He needed to go to the bank and transfer his savings and checking accounts to his name alone. How dreadful that task would be for him. But he knew he needed to do it. And yet he was so befuddled that he had even forgotten where he was going. This kind of memory gap can be alarming to a person, but especially to one who is grieving.

Cognitive function is defined as the intellectual process by which one becomes aware of, perceives, or comprehends ideas. Cognitive function embraces the quality of knowing, which includes all aspects of perception: recognition, conception, sensing, thinking, reasoning, remembering, and imagining. Cognitive impairment is the difficulty in dealing with or reacting to new or novel information or situations.[2]

Such is the state of thinking and cognitive indications that a person is grieving. Confusion, reduced attention span, forgetfulness, paranoia, compulsiveness, obsessions, hallucinations, all are indications that a person's thinking has been impaired by his or her grief. The mind can become quite confusing in such a way that people may think they're going crazy. But they're not going crazy; they're grieving.

These are some other ways that people can be affected in their minds:

- Loss of focus while reading, distraction during conversation, giving attention to detail at work.
- Loss-centered thinking: focus of much of the individual's thought process to the point of obsessiveness.
- Impaired self-esteem.
- Idealization of the past, of the future, and of the individual and the relationship lost.
- Exaggerations in magical thinking (I made it happen).

A leader is in a position to encourage grievers to think beyond themselves. They can ask some probing questions that will help grievers to focus and think beyond their present circumstances. What is it that they are good at and like to do? What purpose has God given to them? How can they help somebody else? Many times, when individuals can look beyond them-

---

2. See www.drgeorgepc.com/MEDMemoryCognitivel; accessed October 30, 2014.

selves, it helps with them to step outside their situation and see things more clearly.

One dear elderly woman who was much beloved in a church I served, had suffered the loss of her husband many years earlier. She was over-wrought with grief, especially since he died so suddenly. She could still remember so vividly: "Big Harold just laid down on the couch and died." It was such a shock. Not long thereafter, Ms. Deonie said that she got a grip on herself. She decided the only way to survive was to get outside of herself. So, she began to bake coffee cakes and take them to shut-ins, church members who were grieving, families that were hurting—just about anyone who needed a lift! Ms. Deonie became renowned for her coffee cakes, and even I became a recipient on several occasions. She said it kept her from going crazy, and along with her faith, gave her another reason to get up and get going each day.

Helping persons to reach beyond themselves and engage in healthy activities is another way to encourage their cognitive processes. Encourage the person to go for a daily walk. One half-hour of walking each day is good for the body, but it is also excellent for the mind. There is something special about getting out in nature, seeing the trees, enjoying the fresh air, watching small animals at play, chatting with people in one's neighbor-hood. If people can do that each day, it will have a positive effect on their mind and overall attitude.

The leader's role is to do what can be done to encourage positive thinking and nurture healing of the mind. It will take some time, but gentle prodding and positive reinforcement will help to move them to-ward hope and healing.

SOCIAL

Georgia had spent most of the last three years in the bedroom, only com-ing out for brief periods to eat and mingle with her family. She had lost her husband by death, and was overwrought with grief. In the process, she had become a veritable recluse, and had withdrawn from her church, her friends, her neighbors, and her community. But one day it dawned upon her that she was not getting any better. She knew that she was stuck in her grief. She had been invited recently to a grief support group. She decided to make herself attend one meeting, thinking it might bring some help that she desperately needed. She shared that it did make a difference. She began to respond to others in the group, and became more receptive to the counsel and comfort that was there. While she still struggled, she made progress in her life and in the socialization that was needed to assist her in her grief journey.

One of the most necessary aspects in our lives is relationships and the connections we make with other people. We are sociable creatures by nature, and when those connections are interrupted, we experience a major disconnect that impacts us dramatically. Some of us may retreat into isolation like Georgia did. It is a time that a leader can reach out to people and encourage them to nurture their relationships with family, friends, and others who have been part of their lives.

Social behavior can reflect what Georgia experienced, or it may go to the other end of the spectrum with over-reaching in social hyperactivity and behavior. Remembering that loss changes people, social reactions can vary related to someone's personality, and what someone is experiencing in the throes of grief.

- Aggressive behaviors reflected in tone of voice, irritability, acting out, raging, tenseness.
- Reckless or self-destructive behaviors: sexual promiscuity, turning to drugs/alcohol, careless driving.
- Turning inward/withdrawing; becoming quiet and introspective; yes or no answers; brief conversation; becoming a recluse.
- Inability to make decisions; apathetic; doubting self; wanting to give up; lacking motivation.
- Excessive activity: throwing themselves into multiple projects, overworking, hyper-verbal activity, trying to get attention.

A leader may be called upon to help individuals who are not responding to their grief in a socially acceptable manner. If they are becoming reclusive, they may need someone to help them focus outward, someone who can befriend the griever and foster positive social activity. If individuals are acting out and engaging in reckless behavior, families may ask the leader to talk with them, help to reel them in, counsel them about the repercussions of their behavior. Let them vent; reassure them regarding self-esteem and worthiness. Pray with them. Share from your own experience. The relationship may be key to opening them to connections that will help them in their grief journey. Their progress will foster their own care and concern for others.

SPIRITUALLY

Recently, I was invited to lead a meeting for grieving persons in a local church. There were people there who had experienced all kinds of losses—spouses, children, parents, siblings. And, they were all ages as well. It reminded me that death is no respecter of persons, and there is plenty of grief to go around. I spoke directly to them about the various misconceptions that people have about grief, then opened it up for questions. There was dead silence. I thought it was "a wrap." And then all of a sudden this lady piped up, "Well, heaven's got to be a great place because this life is pure hell!" I asked several probing questions about her loss, and she revealed that her husband had been killed in a head-on collision with a drunk driver. She was very angry and much of her anger was directed toward God. I did not respond by correcting her thinking, but sought to listen to her pain. I then spoke to the group about being honest with God in their grief. God already knows how one feels, and it is useful to get it out in the open. That paves a way for communication with God, which is essential to the spiritual relationship.

Persons in grief, even persons of great faith, may question God. And there are some grievers who may even wonder if there is a God. Above all, they may want to know why? And why now? And why did it happen to them? They may believe that God has been unfair in taking their loved one, or that they are being punished. There are many statements that are often heard in the church when death comes. "Well, he's in a better place." "You should be happy that she's now at peace." At the time, It

> Grieving allows us to heal, to remember with love rather than pain. It is a sorting process. One by one you let go of things that are gone and you mourn for them. One by one you take hold of the things that have become a part of who you are and build again.
> —Rachael Naomi Remen

may provide little comfort when someone reminds grievers that their loved one is in heaven. All they can think about is how sad they are, and how much they are missing the person. They may be thinking, "Well, it's great that they're in heaven, but I'd rather have them here with me." And they would like someone to understand what they are feeling.

Death and loss is a time when people are called to draw upon their faith. When Christian author Corrie ten Boom was a young girl, and her family was hiding Jewish persons in her home during World War II, she was frightened. Feeling great anxiety, Corrie asked her father if she would have faith when the Nazis came and he was taken away. She recounts:

> I burst into tears, "I need you!" I sobbed. "You can't die! You can't!" "Corrie," he began gently. "When you and I go to Amsterdam, when do I give you your ticket?" "Why, just before we get on the train." "Exactly. And our wise Father in heaven knows when we're going to need things, too. Don't run out ahead of him, Corrie. When the time comes that some of us will have to die, you will look into your heart and find the strength you need just in time."[3]

It's not unusual for grievers to doubt certain things about their faith when death invades their life. Doubt can often lead to greater faith. But people needs those around them who will let them vent, and given the opportunity, seek to meet that doubt in ways that will encourage revived trust and faith in God.

I know when my father died, that I rejoiced that he was in heaven. But, in some ways, as I reflected on his life, I was sad. Don't get me wrong; my father was a courageous leader, and was faithful in his calling as a pastor. But, his terrible fall from a roof at age sixty-two, with subsequent brain damage, lying in a coma for five weeks, spending fourteen months in a rehabilitation center—all of that was very hard for my family, especially my mother. Finally, my dad was able to return home, but his physical and mental capacities were greatly diminished. And now the roles were reversed. My mother had to manage the household, do everything

---

3. Writings from Corrie Ten Boom, http://www.ecclesia.org/truth/corrie.html; accessed October 30, 2014.

in the home and garden, and take care of my dad. My prayer was a very simple one. "Bring him back" I prayed repeatedly every day. And, dad did come back to a certain extent. He was never able to preach again, but he constantly gave witness to his faith. And God graced him with a special sweetness, especially to my mom. He loved everybody he met. He prayed often every day. He would tell me when I called that he had prayed for all three of my children by name. Those are precious memories that lift my spirit when thinking about my dad.

Finally, after thirteen years following his accident, my dad's heart gave way, and he died at the age of seventy-five. But, the last time I went to see him, he ministered to me more than I ministered to him. He reached out in love, embraced me, and we shed many tears together. It was a special time that I will always remember. As I reflected on some of the hardships of my dad's life, I fleetingly wondered "Why?" But, then, I understood that the calling to serve God does not guarantee a bed of roses. In fact, there is suffering, and much of the New Testament speaks to this in a most dramatic way. It was the apostle Paul who wrote: "I want to know Christ—yes, to know the power of his resurrection and participation in his sufferings" (Phil. 3:10, NIV). My dad had suffered, but he also experienced a most sweet fellowship with his Savior. That was reflected in his life in good times, and in hard times as well. And for that, I am grateful. I look forward to seeing him again one day when we are rejoicing together in the presence of the Lord, and all the questions of life will have faded in the perfect understanding and knowledge that we will possess in heaven.

Just as I have grown through my experiences, all leaders have the opportunity to nurture individuals from their own experiences with grief, offering spiritual insight and understanding related to their loved one's death. Besides the counsel they might give from their own experience, they can encourage participating in worship, daily Bible reading, and times of prayer. Following are some other practical ways that grievers can be helped in drawing aside to gain light and hope to in their situation.

- Begin each day with a time of devotion and prayer. Utilizing a devotional book, along with Scripture, is a meaningful way to put one's mind in a good place, and give positive perspective at the outset of one's morning. The Psalms especially provide a wonderful way for persons to pray, even when they don't feel like doing so. The prayers of David are a great comfort, and it helps people to move closer to a time when they feel like communicating with God.

- Look for a special place to pray. The Bible talks about going in your closet, but most of us would find that difficult given the stuff that's already filled it! When I was a boy, we lived on a farm in Maryland, and my dad would go up on the hill behind our house to pray. It was a special place where he met God, and I remember noting often the radiance of Moses when he came off that hill. It was a very special meeting time and place that seemed to transform his countenance and disposition. As a boy, that made a great impression on understanding of the need to draw aside with the Lord.

- Walk with God. Taking a walk, meditating on a Scripture verse, lifting others to the Lord, can be very meaningful and beneficial to one's spiritual life. The Bible talks about Enoch, who walked with God. The fellowship was so sweet and the relationship was so close that one day they walked so far, and the Bible says that Enoch walked right into eternal fellowship with God. What a blessing that would be!

Above all, leaders want to encourage the persons under their leadership in their spiritual journey of faith. Alan Wolfelt calls grief "a soul-based journey." Indeed, it is a meaningful time to draw upon the strengths of faith and turn to God for solace and comfort. As leaders represent the divine presence in their lives, grievers can be encouraged from the Scriptures and from their leaders' own personal experiences with grief.

CONCLUSION

As mentioned in the beginning of this chapter and demonstrated in the five different realms of a person's grief experience, the whole person is affected by loss. How people handle the resulting impact will determine their positive movement forward in rebuilding their lives. The process is not limited to a certain period of time, but the reconciliation to one's grief is related to many different factors. It is an arduous journey for sure, and will take all the resources necessary to deal with the issues. Determination, persistence, courage, faith, patience, perspective, attitude—all these and more attributes enable grieving persons to move from hopelessness to hopefulness in their grief journey. A leader may be called upon to "be there" for a person in many different ways. The leader's own sense of balance in ministry is important in being able to relate to grieving persons. One needs to take care of oneself. Accessing available resources on grief is most helpful. In this way, one is better equipped to provide the guidance and counsel that is needed.

PART II

COMPETENCY IN GRIEF

CHAPTER THREE

DEALING WITH THE FALLACIES OF GRIEF

"The last enemy to be destroyed is death."
(1 Corinthians 15:26, NIV)

We live in a world of continual myths. One goes like this: "If you go outside in the freezing weather without a coat, you'll catch your death of cold!" We've all heard that one before. There are many fallacies in life that people often accept as true. As far as colds go, a cold is caused by a virus, not by a change in temperature. Still, you might contribute to lowering your resistance if you expose yourself to freezing temps for any length of time. How about this one? "If you crack your knuckles, you'll get arthritis!" They researched this old tale, testing three hundred people, and found that cracking your knuckles does not cause arthritis. In fact, normal usage of the hands is a greater risk for arthritis than cracking one's knuckles. But, we all know that it is an annoying habit, and you certainly wouldn't want to irritate everyone around you.

Another fallacy that's passed around goes like this—"If you swallow your chewing gum, your insides will stick together and gum you up!" My aunt tried to convince me of that one. I used to swallow my gum all the time as a little boy. She also told me that if I played with my belly button, my legs would fall off! I was scared to death to touch it for years! I'm glad they were both wrong. Actually, chewing gum acts as a laxative and no doubt moves quicker through your system than anything else! And still another truism, "An apple a day keeps the doctor away." Well, it might if you throw one at her. Although, there is some evidence that suggests that eating apples can reduce the incidence of colon and rectal cancer.

In the realm of grief, there are also many fallacies that are commonly believed in our culture today. While there are perhaps too many more than I have space to elucidate, it is useful to point out some specific ones that tend to predominate in the surrounding culture. As we help grieving people experience healing, it means being engaged in some truth-telling that affects their belief system and journey toward wholeness once again.

FALLACY ONE: You Have to Stay Busy!

"Busy, busy, busy!" is the order of the day for many grievers who find themselves at the receiving end of free advice from their families and friends. "You gotta get out of the house!" "The last thing you want to do is to stay at home and dwell on it!" One lady in a grief group said she was trying to outrun her grief, running as fast she could. She believed the best way to do it was to stay super busy. If she could just fill her life with all kinds of activities and be pre-occupied with lots of other things, then she wouldn't have to focus on her grief. Another man said all he could do was to work, work, work, in order to keep grief off of his mind. He would get up early, go in to work early, work as late as possible, drag himself home, wolf down a TV dinner, and fall into bed. He did this repeatedly for months. Then one day he suddenly realized that he wasn't getting any better. He was stuck in his grief. Trying to outwork or outrun one's grief doesn't work.

The Bible tells us that the last great enemy is death. As Christians, we believe that death was destroyed by the atoning death of Christ. In that death, he overcame death, sin, and the grave. The confidence we have is that one day there will be no more death. Meanwhile, we live on earth and have to face the intrusion of death in our lives when we lose those closest to us. So, discovering ways to work through that grief in this realm is important for us to continue to live lives of purpose and meaning.

We understand that grief is one of the most difficult challenges we face in this life. Once one is struck by it, one may feel stuck in it. You cannot flee from it, you cannot avoid it, and it feels unbearable if you try and embrace it. Leaders or counselors may be called upon to help those who are running away from grief. Leaders need someone to help grievers to stop and realize what is happening. Unless they begin to work through their issues and learn about the importance of mourning, the grief will only inwardly intensify and erupt in other quirky ways in their lives. Grievers should be counseled to lean toward their grief, take some time to fully feel the emotions and intensity of it. Help them to consider the multiple feelings they have, to give ownership to them, and to face them head on. The key is not to stay busy, the key is to have balance. The goal is equilibrium. Sometimes it is important to get outside oneself, and do things that help one to be occupied. Other times it is necessary for them to indulge their grief with all its emotions. One mother shared that after her husband died, "The kids moved in. A year later they moved out. Then my grief hit me like a brick wall." Her grief was delayed, but it came back with a vengeance once the avoidance was removed. The best way to handle grief is go through it, not around it. True healing comes when all the components of grief are realized and experienced in the grief journey.

FALLACY TWO: Grief Is a Five-Step Program

A predominant belief that has reigned for the past forty years or so is that you have to go through a five-step process in the correct order to get over your grief. This idea goes back to the research and classic work of Elisabeth Kübler-Ross, titled *On Death and Dying*. This text was a requirement in the pastoral care studies of my seminary. What we learned was that Dr. Kübler-Ross had conducted a great deal of research with patients who had terminal illnesses and were facing imminent death. She discovered that they went through a process that included denial, anger, bargaining, depression and finally acceptance—in that order. What she didn't realize and what subsequently occurred, was that her work in anticipatory grief would be transferred over to normal grief for survivors after a person died. While there is great merit in Dr. Kübler-Ross's work, she later acknowledged that grief does not occur in a nice orderly fashion.

What Dr. Kübler-Ross acknowledged is in line with the thinking of Russell Friedma, executive director of the Grief Recovery Institute in Sherman Oaks, California, in the book he coauthored titled *The Grief Recovery Handbook* (HarperCollins, 1998). He states:

> No study has ever established that stages of grief actually exist, and what are defined as such can't be called stages. Grief is the normal and natural emotional response to loss.... No matter how much people want to create *simple,*

bullet-point guidelines for the human emotions of grief, there are no stages of grief that fit any two people or relationships.[1]

In reality, grief can occur in a most sporadic manner, and is often related to the unique experience of each person who is grieving the loss of a loved one. To cite a relevant example of grief order gone amuck, an incident occurred recently while I was speaking to a church group composed of many different people with different losses in their lives. As I was addressing this topic, I mentioned that not everyone becomes angry in their grief. A lady in the middle of the group shot

> I led a grief group of seventh graders in my school, and shared the steps of grief with them. I asked them if the order was correct. They said, "No, they're in circles and all happen at 'different times."
> —A middle-school teacher

up her arm and exclaimed, "I am so relieved that you just said that!" She had been told by a well-meaning friend that if she had not been angry, then she had not really grieved. It had plagued her for months. While stage-based models are informative, they are not the last word.

FALLACY THREE: Grief Is Something to "Get Over"

A popular mind-set related to grief is that it is something to be overcome rather than experienced. People often ask me, "When will this pain end?" "How long will I be hurting?" "Does it ever get better?" A helpful analogy perhaps is one that compares the oscillating intensity of grief to the experience of walking into the ocean. As you meet the close crashing waves and feel the force of their frequency and intensity, so grief is like that. It smacks you in the face and threatens to knock you over. But as you go farther out, the waves are less intense, and do not occur as frequently. While you may have one huge wave surprise you every once in a while, there is more calmness and fewer whitecaps that you encounter. Grief

---

1. Cited at http://www.griefrecoverymethod.com/press/five-fallacies-of-grief-debunking-psychological-stages/ accessed October 14, 2014

may be like that—in time the pain does lessen, but the grief will never completely leave you.

Contrary to popular opinion, there is no finish line for grief. The reality is that one never gets over their grief completely. Rather than use the words "resolution," "recovery," or "closure," it is better to use a more meaningful term—reconciliation. There is a certain finality that comes with the other words. Reconciliation, however, doesn't speak to getting over one's grief, but reconciling oneself to it, and integrating it into your life. A person who experiences loss of a loved one is a changed person, forever. One young lady lamented how hurt she felt when, after expressing grief to a friend with many tears, the friend responded, "I'll be glad when you get back to your old self!" She would have loved to do just that. But people cannot will themselves back to a time when life was different, when their loved one was with them. The old normal is gone, the person is not coming back, and steps must be taken to manage the change that has foisted itself on a person's life. In the Bible, we see the example of King David, who grieved heavily after the death of his son Absalom. His life was never the same; grief remained in his household and stayed with him till his dying day.

Grief is not an illness from which someone must recover. It is a process in which a person experiences change and transformation over a period of time. When individuals lose loved ones, they lose part of themselves. Their lives are now different; the old normal has passed, and they must discover a new normal. While they no longer have the physical presence of their loved ones, they now have a relationship of memory and emotion. As they learn to accommodate themselves to the loss, there comes healing and growth that leads to a deeper, more meaningful life.

FALLACY FOUR: Faith Makes Grieving Easy

Persons who have a strong faith will readily tell you, "I don't know what I would do if I didn't have my faith." Time and time again I've heard people share the importance of their faith in dealing with grief. When they think of their loved one in heaven, it is a great source of comfort and strength. The peace of mind that is felt in knowing about a person's eternal destination is priceless. For those who are unsure, we must remember that God is the final judge. Eternal matters must be placed in his hands.

Unfortunately, there are some proponents of a "new science" in thanatology who debunk the whole concept of heaven. Secular psychologist

George Bonano in his book *The Other Side of Sadness* has this to say about heaven in relation to grief: "Probably the biggest stumbling block, whether we are actively religious or not, is that heaven just doesn't hold up as a believable concept."[2] While there may be some helpful insights in Bonano's book, his churlish notion about relegating belief in heaven to only the poor and less-educated people of the world displays an incredible ignorance about its importance also to millions of educated grieving people around the globe. This so-called "new science" approach seems rather a tired and scientifically unreliable source of misinformation regarding eternal truths, as well as other important components of the grief process.

As stated earlier, Dr. Alan Wolfelt, noted grief author and educator, calls grief a "soul-based journey." Indeed, every part of a person—mind, body, and spirit is involved in the grieving process. And faith is a huge component in that journey. Still, sometimes, there are unreal expectations of grievers by other religious believers who have not experienced the same loss themselves. In their attempts to comfort and identify with the griever, it appears as if they may be minimizing the loss. They will say "Well, he's in a better place." Yes, he is, but he is missed greatly and the griever would still like him to be here. "You should be happy that she's not in any more pain." Yes, that's true. But the griever's pain in grief is stifling. "Just turn it over to God, and everything will be all right." Easily said, but it is the griever who is feeling the burden in spite of all efforts to release it to God.

Sometimes, the insensitivity of fellow Christians can be quite painful. While they are well-meaning, they certainly can put their foot in it at times. One person, seeking to comfort a fellow church member who had lost her son in a tragic auto accident, said without thinking, "Well, at least he didn't suffer; he is in heaven, and you don't know what he was spared!" The mother was crushed by such a crass and flippant statement. Another lady said that she was so upset with her church, their insensitivity to her loss, and their reticence in reaching out to her. Finally, days later, when the deacons turned up at her door, she told them they were too late. There is much to be learned about the role of faith and its application to grief. But there are no shortcuts to grieving, and faith does not make it a simple easy task, though it can make a significant difference in the long term.

---

2. George Bonano, *The Other Side of Sadness: What the New Science of Bereavement Tells Us About Life after Loss* (New York: Basic Books, 2009), 148.

FALLACY FIVE: Grievers Are Weak If They Question Their Faith

The onset of grief can bring grievers to a point of crisis in their faith. When a traumatic loss occurs, that world is shattered. A person's sense of self-worth is damaged, life appears to be meaningless and hopeless, and the world no longer seems benevolent and safe. The rebuilding of that world can take a great deal of time, with hard work and plenty of support. But even then, the world is not put back together exactly the same way as before. There is a new perception of the word—persons who grieve are a little less confident and a little less sure of all the things they once believed to be true and certain.

A significant loss challenges all of a person's basic beliefs about the nature and fairness of the universe, the existence of a higher power, or even the very nature of God. So obviously there may be questions related to faith and even doubt about God's goodness and loving intentions. Rather than fight the process, it may be best for the leader to offer unconditional love, exercise patience and compassion, and gently lead those grieving toward finding their way and having their faith restored.

> A Christian man may stand and weep; he may kiss the dear cold hand for the last time and rain showers of tears on the lifeless body while "pity swells the tide of love."… He may sorrow—he ought to.…Yet we may not, and we must not, weep as others weep. *"We grieve, but not as those who have no hope."*
> —C. H. Spurgeon

Unfortunately, persons who question their faith in the throes of grief are often considered weak by other people of faith. I grew up in a family where I was told that you never question God. I had a healthy fear of my father, and I wasn't about to question him! But to me, questioning God did not seem quite as threatening. As best as I tried to receive my dad's counsel with my head, I could not grasp it with my heart. I discovered later that Job questioned God many times. Although God did not directly answer his questions, Job was as a man of rejuvenated faith experienced restoration and new beginnings.

I believe it is good for people to be honest with God. It's not like God doesn't already know what one is thinking! And, I think God can handle the questions and the doubts. Doubt often leads to greater faith. Individuals working through their questions can come out much stronger at the other end. As Helen Keller once stated: "I do not want the peace that passeth understanding. I want the understanding which bringeth peace." We need to offer the peace and understanding of Christ to those who are experiencing questions and doubts as they grieve. Hopefully, they will move positively in the direction of believing once again in the three fundamental assumptions, and their faith in God will become even stronger than before.

FALLACY SIX: Time Heals All Wounds

You've heard it said often that "time heals all wounds." Not so fast, my friend. There are different kinds of times, and time by itself does nothing. It just passes. It is what you do with the time that counts. Grief is an adaptive response that is not measured by time. It is something you learn to live with over time. The grief can abate somewhat over time and flare up less often, but can burst into your life without notice on certain occasions. The important thing is to make meaningful choices that help grievers move positively in their lives.

In her article "How Long Is This Grief Going to Last?" grief author Elizabeth Harper Neeld speaks about two different kinds of time: *chronos* time and *kairos* time.[3] *Chronos* time is the kind that relates to the ticking of the clock, and to the calendar. *Kairos* time has to do with "the time within which personal life moves

> Don't let anyone take your grief away from you. You deserve it, and you must have it. If you had major surgery, no one would pressure you to run in a marathon the next week. Grief is a major wound. It does not heal overnight. You must take the time and use the crutches until you heal.
> —Doug Manning, *Don't Take My Grief Away*

---

3. Cited at http://www.examiner.com/article/time-kairos-or-chronos; accessed October 30, 2014.

forward." *Kairos* has to do with certain awakenings within moments of our lives that brings realization. It is not a measured time, but it is an ordered time. What insights have grievers had in their grief? What have they realized? What meaning are they able to make of their terrible loss?

Time that is well spent usually lessens the intensity of the feelings. The "firsts" can be difficult: marking the first Christmas without the person, the first New Year's, or the first birthday. For many people, having gone through a year without a loved one is a milestone. According to Neeld, however, it may not be useful to measure one's grieving in *chronos* time. There may be a false assessment of the time that has passed and the progress one has made in one's grief. In reality, the amount of *kairos* time it takes individuals to reach a point where their loss has become integrated into their lives is longer than a "person on the street" might think. The important concept to remember is that one's healthy grieving is not dependent on *chronos* time. It does happen all in good time. All in good *kairos* time.

FALLACY SEVEN: The Goal Is to Let Go of Your Loved One and Move on with Life

The lament that is shared in David Gates' song Everything I Own expresses the sentiments of many persons who have lost a loved one to death. Gates wrote the song for his father, who had died a short time before, expressing the sentiment that he would give everything he owned, just to have him back again.

While the world may be short-sighted when it comes to urging a family member or friend to let go of his or her loved one and move on with life, it's exactly the opposite of what the griever feels.

I knew one couple who lost their teenage son who was killed in a head-on collision with a large truck while returning to college. They were utterly devastated. They intended to preserve everything about his life, making a shrine out of his room, leaving everything as it was when he died. This went on for a long period of time. Then they experienced a dramatic reversal. They invited a young man to stay in their home who was serving in a local ministry. They allowed him to stay in the son's room. It began a healing process that enabled them to move forward with their lives. But they did not let go of their son's memory. They still remembered him; they still loved him; they still cherished his life.

Sandy Goodman writes:

> We have not done well with dying. We have denied its re-
> ality and considered it an end to life that should be avoid-
> ed at all costs. We tell our children that Grandma died
> and went to a beautiful place called Heaven, and then we
> quit saying her name. We cart her clothes off to the Salva-
> tion Army, sell her house, cry (but only in secret) when
> someone inadvertently mentions her, and put all the pic-
> tures into storage. Instead of seeing death as the next stage
> of life and exploring the possibilities of such a belief, we
> choose to let fear keep us ignorant.[4]

Sandy touches on an important reality. You don't divorce yourself from
a person's memory and cut that individual out of your life. That is brutal
and unthinkable.

The relationship of love is not severed by death, but the positive nature of that relationship is continued in a manner that will honor the
person's life and continue the bonds throughout a lifetime. Even though
a person is no longer physically present, the emotional component of love
continues. If people stop grieving, they may be fearful of stopping the
love for their dear ones. One man said, "I've closed the gate, but I haven't
left her behind. I've just moved on in a meaningful way." It is not morbid
or sickly to want to maintain a bond with someone who has died. Rather
it is positive and healthy to foster the cherished memories that will help
to sustain a person in the days to come. The relationship is not the same,
but it is a meaningful one nevertheless.

Bruce Horacek challenged the common assumption that the main
task of grieving is a "detaching" of emotional connections to the loved
one who has died. He poses an alternative model in which a person
grieving may be able to make the necessary adjustments to functioning
in everyday life. But their world is not where the deceased loved one is
left behind. They embrace a different relationship and are able to grow
with their new perspective. So, for the grieving person, it is not a matter

---

4. Cited at http://innerself.com/content/spirituality/death-a-dying/4889-i-didnt-know-about-
   death-by-sandy-goodman.html; accessed October 30, 2014.

of letting go and moving on. It is a matter of change, adapting to that change, and carrying the relationship forward in a positive manner.[5]

CONCLUSION

There are many false beliefs and fallacies related to grief that could not be covered in this chapter. Leaders do well to consider their own thoughts and beliefs about some of the following statements that are made by uninformed persons in regard to the reality of grief and its manifestation in a griever's life. Look at the statements below offered by Dr. Therese Rando and decide how many of them you believe.[6]

- All losses are similar.
- It only takes two months to move past the death of a loved one.
- All people grieving do it in the same way.
- Grief declines regularly over time.
- Once you are over your grief, it never resurfaces.
- Family will always be there to help you through loss.
- Adults and children grieve in similar was.
- Do not feel sorry for yourself.
- It's better not to think about painful experiences.
- No one should think about their deceased loved ones during the holidays.
- All you need to do is express your feelings and you'll resolve your grief.
- Expressing intense feelings means you're losing control.
- It is wrong to express anger at someone as long as those people were doing their best.
- It is wrong to express anger toward your deceased loved one.
- Having physical problems in grief means you're sick.
- If you feel crazy it means you are crazy.
- The only emotion you should feel when someone you loved dies is sadness.

---

5. Bruce Horacek, "Toward a More Viable Model of Grieving and Consequences for Older Persons," *Death Studies* (Washington DC: Hemisphere Publishing Corporation, vol 15.5, 1991).
6. Adapted from Therese A. Rando, *How to Go on Living When Someone You Love Dies* (New York: Bantam Books, 1991), 6–9.

- You should be able to move on from the death of an infant because you didn't know the child for very long.
- You should keep children' from grieving and protect them from death.
- Grieving the death of a loved one is a sign that you lack faith in God and don't trust your religion.
- Eventually everything will return to the way things were before your loved one died.
- After someone dies, you will no longer have a relationship with that individual.
- How much you loved your loved one correlates with how intense your grief happens to be.
- You should be happy your other family members are still alive, so there's something wrong if you don't feel close to them anymore..
- You should never think that a part of you died along with your loved one.
- Losing a spouse is exactly the same as losing a child.
- Clichés are always the best thing to use if you don't necessarily know what to say to someone who lost a loved one.
- Grief has to do with losing a person from your life and nothing else.
- The only affect grief will have on you is psychological.
- All widows should grieve in the same way.
- Death is death. It doesn't matter if you anticipate it or not.
- If your parent dies when you are an adult it isn't as traumatic as it would be if you are a child.
- After a couple's child dies, divorce is almost always inevitable.
- Social support for your grief is great, but not necessary.
- The best thing to do when someone dies is to put that person in your past and not focus on him or her..
- You can avoid the pain of grief and still resolve your grief successfully.

While a leader may be attempting to resonate with the what-to-do's and the what-not-to-do's in handling fallacies about grief, it is best to remember that the most important thing one has to offer is one's presence. Words can be cheap. Most importantly, the leader is not there primarily to teach about grief in that moment, but to become a learner from the ones who are grieving. This insight is one of the best teachings to come out of the writings of Elisabeth Kübler-Ross. It means that rather than having a systematic approach to all grieving situations, it is rather more profitable to allow the people one serves and counsel to lead from their experience. They are the experts at what they are feeling and going through, not the leader or anyone else. The best leader will be willing to listen and learn. Then, appropriate guidance may be offered, clarifying the fallacies that often arise through misinformation.

CHAPTER FOUR

THE SPINNING WHEEL OF CHOICES

*I am now giving you the choice between life and death ... and I
call heaven and earth to witness the choice you make. Choose life.*
Deuteronomy 30:19, GNT

Imagine what it would be like to have written a best-selling book
that has helped to change millions of lives, as well as leading a church
where thousands have come to faith. That experience might be the envy
of many leaders. But then, consider how difficult it would be for that
same person to wake up one day and discover that his son had died by
suicide. No one would want that experience. Such is the case of Rick
Warren, world-famous pastor of Saddleback Church, who wrote *The Purpose Driven Life*, a book that has inspired many people to seek faith and
experience transformation in their lives. Recently, Rick experienced a different sort of transformation, the unenviable life change that comes with
losing a child. That became evident when he appeared with his wife Kay
on "Piers Morgan Tonight" on CNN to talk about their son Matthew.
After twenty-seven years of suffering with a personality disorder, Matthew
had taken his own life. Rick lamented: "The day that I had feared might
happen, one day, since he'd been born, and the day that I prayed would
never happen, happened." Rick and Kay's story of their family's tireless efforts to help their son is moving, and their faith in the midst of their grief
is inspiring. They chose to go public with their story so that they might
bring greater awareness to mental health issues, and help other families

who are coping with loved ones who suffer from mental disorders. Their courageous choice to grieve through social media has helped millions of families, and given them a way to turn their personal tragedy toward the positive goal of bringing hope to others.

Grieving people face many choices. For them, some of the normal choices that people make on a daily basis become very difficult. Sometimes, grievers can only function in a survival mode mustering barely enough energy to drag themselves out of bed. Even in the midst of grief at its worst, however, individuals who seek healing from their loss must deal with the choices before them. These choices may be critical to a griever's health and well-being. One's motivation, attitude, determination, resilience—comprise a mind-set affecting choices that are not always quantifiable but real nevertheless. While it was not the survivor's choice when it came to losing a loved one, grievers are then forced to make choices that will have ramifications for the rest of their life. Leaders are in a position to help bring clarity and provide guidance to people they know who are dealing with difficult decisions.

THE WHEEL OF CRITICAL CHOICES

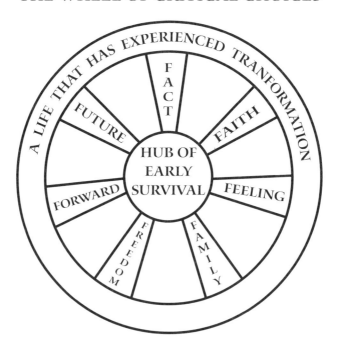

It is important to note that the grief process is not linear, but is more often experienced in cycles. Grief is sometimes compared to climbing a spiral staircase where things can look and feel like you are just going in circles, yet you are actually making progress. Being patient with the process and allowing yourself to have any feelings about the loss can help. If you feel stuck in your grief, talking to a counselor or a supportive person may help you move forward in the healing process.

Many years ago when I was a teenager, the popular song "Spinning Wheel" by the group Blood, Sweat & Tears grabbed my attention. In addition to the upbeat jazzy melody, the words were pithy and thought-provoking.[1]

Imagine if you will a "spinning wheel" of grief that is ever-moving and constantly in motion. Then think about a person who is grieving and facing all kinds of choices. In this analogy the person moves from the hub to the spokes of different choices. While there is progression as the wheel spins, the person choosing is moving back and forth to different spokes, yet moving forward at the same time. The wheel has a hub, and that hub is early survival. The spokes represent choices that will direct the griever toward hope and healing. The outside rim represents a life that has experienced transformation. It can be a meaningful and productive journey on the way to new beginnings. Leaders will learn to recognize these choices and thus be enabled to connect and give guidance to grievers as they face the critical choices before them.

THE HUB OF EARLY SURVIVAL

Critical choices face grievers from day one, when the impact of their loved one's death comes crashing down upon them. Most of those choices relate to immediate responsibilities related to funeral preparations and the immediate aftermath. At this time, individuals in the throes of grief may not be totally cognizant of decisions they are making. It's all about survival. To survive, a person who is grieving the loss of a loved one has to slog through the arduous early days of frenetic emotions. Elizabeth Harper Neeld, the author of the classic grief work

---

1. http://www.oldielyrics.com/lyrics/blood_sweat_tears/spinning_wheel.html; accessed October 30, 2014.

Seven Choices, was invited to speak at our local fundraiser. She shared gripping stories about the difficult choices she had to make as a young widow when her husband suddenly died while taking an afternoon jog. In her book, she was amazingly honest, bearing her soul and not hiding all the machinations of her grueling journey toward loving life again. Ten years later, after working through much of her grief and experiencing growth in creating a new life, she penned a book that has helped thousands of people. In fact, the book was distributed by The Red Cross to grief counselors working with surviving families of the 9/11 attack on the World Trade Center in New York. Elizabeth's experience shows that grievers can navigate their grief from the days of early survival to the point of integration, where they can reconcile themselves to their grief and engage life again.

What are the choices that will lead persons who are grieving toward a new beginning where they can thrive in a new lifestyle without their loved one? Meaningful choices must be directed toward a goal. What is the goal? For Elizabeth Neeld, the goal was to love life again. That is a noble goal. For someone else the goal might be to become a fully functioning person again with a renewed purpose in life. It all begins with the right attitude. "Individuals have the ability to make choices, including the choice of the attitude they adopt."[2] To make positive choices, people must have a positive attitude. They can choose either to directly face their grief head-on, or bury their heads in the sand and seek to avoid it altogether. But the choice comes down to

> Volition, or choice, is the exercise of the will, the capacity of the person to *originate* things and events that would not otherwise be or occur.
> —Dallas Willard

this: Will the person become a victim or a victor? The healthy choice of working through the grief is a proactive choice that will lead one toward healing. Margaret H. Garner wrote a poem titled "It's My

---

2. Wendy G. Lichtenthal and William Breitbart, "Finding Meaning through the Attitude One Takes" in R.A. Neimeyer (Ed.) *Techniques of Grief Therapy: Creative Strategies for Counseling the Bereaved* (New York: Routledge, 2012), 163).

Choice to Be a Survivor or a Victim" that is helpful in understanding the choices involved.[3]

The hub of survival includes different elements. Of course, it is most difficult at the onset to make choices—so *patience* with oneself is required during these early days. Healthy choices include moving toward the grief process and seeking to be proactive in one's healing. At first, grief is all-consuming, and the pain is overwhelming. Each person is in a state of shock and numb to the core. Some describe this feeling as like being "in a fog," which is the body's way of protecting a person—no one is able to absorb everything all at once and continue to function and survive. But, not long after the shock wears off, each person needs to decide how to handle grief. The choice for health and wholeness means becoming proactive in the grief process. Death is an unwelcome visitor, but those who

> Don't let anyone take your grief away from you. You deserve it, and you must have it. If you had a broken leg, no one would criticize you for using crutches until it was healed. If you had major surgery, no one would pressure you to run a marathon the next week. Grief is a major wound. It does not heal overnight. You must take the time and use the crutches until you heal.
> —Doug Manning,
> *Don't Take My Grief Away*

are bereaved must understand that their response is something within the realm of their control. The greater the active role that is played, the quicker one will move toward healing.

THE SPOKE OF FACT

Choose to face the reality of the death. The horror of death is its finality. The fact is that someone loved has died. The loved one is not coming back. While denying it for a time, a person must come to grips with the

---

3. Poem cited at http://cribsforkids.org/wp-content/uploads/2011/08/Its-My-Choice-to-Be-a-Survivor-or-a-victim.pdf; accessed October 28, 2014.

finality of the death. Choosing to face that reality enables a person to withstand the torrential downpour of grief that comes.

On one occasion, I was at my daughter's softball game, enjoying watching her play at center field and catch some amazing fly balls. She was up to bat, and she took the second pitch with a vengeance, sending it out to the far left field. She raced to first and steamed into second base untouched, the ball flying past the second baseman. Then someone tapped me on the shoulder. It was a church member. Did I know, they asked, that Mrs. Knoll's husband had died suddenly of a heart attack that afternoon, and was found by his wife in the back yard as she returned from the grocery store? I did not know.

As caught up as I was in the game, my position and role called for the immediate leaving of my daughter's game, and rushing over to the home of my church member. When I arrived, Mrs. Knoll was distraught, overcome with her loss, and weeping uncontrollably. It was a sad situation; the death was so abrupt. But there I was once again in my role as a pastor, seeking to bring some measure of comfort and presence to the moment. It was difficult. There were no words that would change what had just happened. I hugged her, and reached out to extend my deepest sympathy, but also felt that familiar feeling of inadequacy that comes when attempting to console someone during such trying circumstances. I listened to her laments, and sought to bring some measure of consolation. One thing I noticed, though: She made an immediate shift from her overwhelming emotions to the necessity of the moment, and the need to make plans for her husband's funeral service. She promptly moved toward encountering her grief, and in the long run, it was the best choice. As time went by, she adapted to her newfound situation and became well-integrated back into life.

What Mrs. Knoll experienced is termed "Impact" by Dr. Elizabeth Neeld. It is the immediate response when a person has learned about a loved one's death. At that moment, an individual's life is changed forever. All the plans, all the dreams, all the hopes for the life a person planned with a loved one are dashed and destroyed. It is an emotional earthquake and shatters one's life in a most dramatic way. In this immediate phase grievers are gripped with disbelief and denial. Emotions are rampant and the tears flow freely for many. Others find it difficult to cry. Still the questions abound. How can it be? How could this happen to them? Why them, why now? All of a sudden, they have to deal with funeral arrangements, memorial services, and all the consternation of seeking to pay final tribute to their loved ones. The denial and shock is a form of God-given protection, enabling grievers to function when otherwise they might succumb to their grief. Leaders are called upon to bring solace and comfort at this critical juncture when grievers face the reality of death invading their life.

THE SPOKE OF FAITH

Choose to exercise one's faith. The critical choice related to faith is essential in the grief journey. A person's faith is important to surviving during the early stages of grief, as well as the days to come. The comfort that comes from experiencing the grace and love of a faith relationship enables a person to have the greater perspective of eternal life. This gives the hope and comfort of a future that is steadfast and sure, according to the promises of God's word. A leader will assist them to call on their personal faith that will help them through the journey that lay ahead. Consider the following elements essential to a vital faith.

Prayer. Communicating with God is a necessary part of engaging one's faith. Oftentimes, people will say to a griever, "You're in my thoughts and prayers." While it may seem a well-worn expression, it can have great significance for the survivor. It signals to the person grieving the dynamic role of prayer, and that it is a significant gesture if offered in truth. A leader can pray with them, and encourage them to become active in their own prayer

> My God, my God, why have you deserted me?... I call all day, my God, but you never answer. All night long I call and cannot rest.... Do not stand aside; trouble is near. I have no one to help me.... Do not stand aside, O God. O my strength, come quickly to my help....
> —Psalm 22

life. Sometimes people don't feel like praying. But, perhaps the most effective prayer is one that cannot be expressed in words. The affections of the heart are evident to a loving God who cares.

Meditation. It's helpful to find a quiet place to reflect and meditate. Perhaps using a daily devotional in a favorite chair where there is solitude will bring much-needed solace. All of this is most helpful in practicing one's faith and drawing strength and help from God. Meditating on the Scriptures provides great consolation in times of distress, especially the Psalms.

Attending worship. Sometimes people draw back from their church or synagogue. Especially if the funeral was held in the church, sometimes it becomes a barrier as it brings back fresh memories that may be painful for a time. Still, others may find comfort in that fact. Leaders may notice someone's absence who has experienced a recent loss. They need to seek out that person, and discover if there are issues related to worship. This is the time to nurture that person, and find friends who will reach out to this person when he or she attends.

One grieving widow explained she had to sit at the back of the church for a while. A man who lost his wife said he could not sit in the same pew. A mother found it most difficult to be in worship without her child. A leader has a unique role in gently encouraging parishioners to share their doubts and fears in an atmosphere of acceptance and understanding.

Some people in grief question their faith and seek to find the "meaning of life" in the depths of their sorrow. They are impacted by their feelings and through a searching process begin to comprehend what has happened in their world. Letting grievers know that they can be honest with God, should they feel abandoned, is also freeing to them. Since God already knows how they feel, their honesty is a step toward restoring the relationship so that their faith can become beneficial in the process of grieving. Even in their inability to comprehend the unanswered questions of their situation, understand perfectly and attain the answers they are looking for, the cries of their wounded soul find respite in foundations of their faith.

A leader may want to encourage a griever to receive the counsel that author Father Joe Phillips offers to those persons who may be dealing with anger toward God (Bereavement Magazine):

- Have it out with God as you would with a friend.
- Write a letter to God.
- Write a letter from God to you, putting into words what God would want to say to you at this time.
- Pray one of the angry Psalms.
- Listen to music while repeating a verse from Scripture.
- Take a long walk with God.
- Ask a friend to listen to how angry you feel.

Viktor Frankl, in his classic work *Man's Search for Meaning,* described how individuals can transcend their circumstances and suffering with the attitude: "He who has a *why* to live can bear with almost any *how*." Every person possesses his or her own source of meaning, which Frankl separated into three distinct directions: "1) by creating a work or doing a deed; 2) by experiencing something or encountering someone; and 3) by the attitude we take toward unavoidable suffering."[4] Those who have faith do not grieve like those who do not possess faith. It makes a real difference in the depth and extent of grief. One is compelled by faith to face forward and do what it takes to let that faith do its work for good.

THE SPOKE OF FEELING

Choose to experience fully the emotions of grief. Feelings are inevitable in life, and certainly prevalent with grief. It is necessary that grievers are encouraged to accept that their emotions are normal, and that they are given permission to feel and express them, regardless of whether they seem good or bad. The emotions are strong and overpowering. But if a person goes down into the depths, they will rise up after working through all that they are feeling at the time.

The emotions of grief are many—sadness, fear, loneliness, love, anger, guilt, abandonment, relief, and hopelessness, to name a few. These emotions are intense and often overwhelming. They collide in a way that generates much consternation on the part of the griever. But it is necessary to allow oneself to own those feelings, and work through them as they arise.

A very effective way to express and release emotions is through tears. Just as laughter enables individuals to give voice to joy, crying is a natural and healthy means of expressing pain and sorrow. While it is commonly said that laughter is the best medicine, tears are equally therapeutic, especially in the realm of grief. Some people, however, are unable to cry. One

> An emotional earthquake has occurred, and the aftershock goes on and on, often feeling as bad or worse than the original quake.
> —*Bereavement Magazine*

---

4. Ibid., 161.

widow in a support group said that she was very upset that she had not been able to cry. People around her did not think she was grieving because she could not cry. On the contrary, the fact that she couldn't cry increased her angst and put additional stress upon her in her grief.

Positive emotions like love, joy, and peace are easier to express and are acceptable to others. It is more difficult to deal with death with negative emotions like fear and anger. They are often unpleasant and awkward. But all emotions at some point need to be released. It is important for them to be released in a manner that is not harmful to self or others. For example, finding a positive outlet for anger is most helpful in dealing with it. Some grievers go out in the woods and scream, others punch a pillow, others go for long walks, still others engage in sports or strenuous activity to release the anger and tension. One man declared that throwing dishes against the basement wall did wonders for his anger!

Some grievers may attempt to dull the emotions through drugs or alcohol. But these are short-term solutions that may develop into dependency and addiction. It is better not to run from the emotions but find constructive ways for them to be experienced as a normal part of one's grief journey.

THE SPOKE OF FAMILY AND SUPPORT

Choose to reach out for help. A circle of support is critical to moving through grief. Having family, friends, work associates, fellow church members, support groups—all enable a person to experience different avenues of support. A person must choose to reach out for help. It doesn't usually come out of the blue, but mostly comes from one's own sphere of loved ones and friends. C. S. Lewis found that after his wife died, his close circle of friends found it difficult to relate to his loss. He needed support, so he searched and found some new friends who understood and offered consolation in the midst of his grief. He was wise enough to know he could not face his journey all by himself.

Another story reveals a source of support that is necessary. A young man was driving his car down the interstate with his cousin alongside in the front seat. The discussion was quite serious. The cousin was distraught over family situations and feeling great rejection. The two had been drinking, and it may have affected the cousin's tragic decision. Out of nowhere, or so it seemed to the driver, the cousin opened the passenger door and jumped out while the car was speeding along. Unfortunately, the injuries were fatal. It was devastating for the driver. The incident resulted in the driver being charged with his cousin's death. He went to prison for three years. He experienced much anger and resentment over his situation. He loved his cousin, and was devastated by what happened. But, nevertheless, he had to go away for a while. While in prison, his wife divorced him. Life seemed to have turned against him. He felt so alone. But he did not lose his faith. In fact, his faith held him in check, and he quietly finished his sentence and returned to the world. After some time, he went to a grief support group. He had grief issues that were still haunting him. The group provided a means for him to share and also receive support from other participants who had lost loved ones.

Attending a grief support group is one effective way for grievers to get in touch with all that they are experiencing in their loss. The group provides a safe place for persons to share their story, talk about their loved one, express emotions, and receive guidance for the journey before them. A leader can help someone by encouraging them to reach out to others for help. Other are garnering support through Facebook groups online and utilizing social media. These efforts should not be discouraged because they provide valuable connections and support.

Reaching out to family and others is not as easy as one would think. So many people have been raised to be independent. People are prone to think "I can handle this grief myself!" It is difficult to ask for help. A leader can recognize their need for help and prod them in the right direction. When one hurts so much, the inertia of grief becomes a roadblock to seeking support. And yet, the understanding and acceptance of those who love and care for a griever is irreplaceable. Drawing from the strength and support that is offered will foster a person's progress in working through one's grief. Grievers need to embrace those who seek to embrace them. They should be urged to step out of their comfort zone and receive help and assistance. The journey is too difficult to go it alone.

Leaders needs to encourage persons who are grieving to take the initiative as much as they can muster their strength. It will take much effort. One way they can lift their spirits and avert chronic depression is by reaching out to others. If there are places they can serve or volunteer, they can be prodded toward becoming involved somewhere so they can get beyond themselves and assist others.

On the other hand, If the situation merits it and the griever is having a very difficult time functioning with grief, he or she should be advised to seek professional help from a counselor or therapist. Typically, a leader cannot provide all the care that someone needs in these extreme situations. But, grievers can be pointed in a direction that will give them tools they need to overcome the obstacles they are facing in their grief.

THE SPOKE OF FREEDOM

Choose to relinquish the past. At some point a person has to drop the baggage with all the nagging questions—Why me? Why my loved one? Why now? Grievers must be relinquished in favor of the "what" and "how" questions. "What now am I going to do with my life?" "How will I go about it?" These are the questions that embrace freedom. Freedom may seem an odd choice when it comes to grief. But in the prospect of charting unknown waters, there are freedoms that arise in the process. Various aspects of one's grief can be relinquished. This is the turning point where decisions must be made about letting go of certain things. At first, it may seem a difficult freedom. Elizabeth Neeld spoke of the unwanted freedom she felt after her husband's untimely death. She wrote: "I was free—within the bounds of my abilities and my resources—to do anything, live anywhere, act any way. But this was freedom that I despised; freedom I did not want; freedom that frightened me."[5] Neeld discovered a freedom that enabled her to begin to turn toward the future. In that way freedom becomes a positive factor focusing on the prospects facing a person.[6]

> There are three needs of the griever: To find the words for the loss, to say the words aloud, and to know that their words have been heard.
> —Victoria Alexander

---

5. Elizabeth Harper Neeld, *Seven Choices: Finding Daylight after Loss Shatters Your World* (New York: Warner Books, 1990), 82.
6. Harold Kuchner's, *When Bad Things Happen to Good People* (New York: Avon Paperbacks, 2004) is a good resource that addresses some of these questions.

Freedom says that a person can choose lots of things, including the company one keeps. Questions a leader might want to ask a survivor— "Who are the people around you, and are they influencing you for good?" Are they being hindered in their movement forward? The Bible says "Bad company corrupts good character" (1 Corinthians 15:33, NIV). In the case of grieving, bad company demoralizes. Unhealthy people can say the wrong things, give the wrong counsel, become critical, negative, demeaning and always questioning one's decisions. Freedom says they might best be avoided. Leaders should counsel individuals to surround themselves with positive persons who will encourage and empower them to move confidently forward. They should steer clear of people who want to tell them what or how to feel.

Freedom says that one doesn't have to go to certain places. Some places bring back painful memories. Some places bring tremendous sadness. They need to be given permission to distance themselves from places that create unnecessary pain.

Freedom says that grievers should avoid certain things: things that create trouble, things that lead to bad choices, things that take them to a bad place. Those things should be avoided. Sad movies, sad stories, tear-jerking novels can bring one right down. They need things that will uplift them and enable them to value the best in life.

Freedom means that a person has the choice to remember the good things, the sweet memories, the special moments that constituted the relationship with the loved one who died. Prioritizing memories is a choice that savors the past in a way that is positive and helpful. One elderly Sunday School teacher shared that when it so happened that the lesson was on human sexuality, she and her widowed class would simply rise and sing together "Precious Memories." Class dismissed.

Freedom says that a griever can choose to enjoy solitude. There is a difference between being alone and being lonely. In choosing solitude, one gives himself /herself the freedom to make meaningful use of time alone—reading a book, taking a walk, engaging in a solo project, meditation/prayer/devotion, etc. Grieving persons can be counseled to seek a place where they be quiet and thoughtful—a particular chair, a favorite room, a setting in nature, a park bench, the back porch. The familiarity and comfort will enhance one's openness toward listening to God and finding solace that is needed.

THE SPOKE OF FORWARD

Choose to adjust to a new assumptive world. In Ronnie Janoff-Bulman's classic book *Shattered Assumptions: Towards a New Psychology of Trauma*, he writes about the way we live in an "assumptive world."[7] In that world we make certain assumptions that are characterized specifically by three beliefs: 1) The world is benevolent, 2) Life is meaningful, 3) The self is worthy. Needless to say, that when one experiences trauma their assumptive worlds are shattered. The world no longer seems safe or benevolent. Life appears meaningless and void of hope. Notions of self-worth suffer and confidence is shaken. The old assumptive world for the griever has been turned upside down.

One widow constantly talked about how she was no longer organized. She had been such an organized person, and now she no longer felt that she could organize anything. Her self-confidence had been rattled. But she was grieving! Another man felt that he was losing his mind. Everything was topsy-turvy. His world was shattered. A mother who lost her child felt frozen in time—her world seemed lost forever. Everyone lives with certain assumptions that they hold to be true. When a loved one dies, many of those assumptions go out the window.

The recovery of the assumptive world occurs with proper support and guidance over a period of time. But the rebuilding of that world does not mean that it is the same again. It has been changed forever. The way one views the world has changed. Purpose and meaning are altered. Relationships are dif-

> Yet some people emerge from their grieving process with unexpected gains. By weathering emotional tribulations they had thought unendurable, they have a deeper, surer sense of their strength. By facing despair, and not succumbing, they know their inner capacities in a more complete way. These gains do not in any way diminish the facts of the loss. But, yes, are benefits. Dearly purchased, hard-earned benefits.
> —Steve Schwartzberg

7. Elizabeth Neeld introduced this concept in her book *Seven Choices,* in the chapter "Second Crisis."

ferent. Assumptions have been revamped and updated. There is a new perception that appreciates the value of life, the significance of what really matters—relationships, family, health, etc. In a sense, the new wisdom is a gift, one that rises out of the ashes of shattered assumptions.

A corollary to this choice is choosing to take steps forward in rebuilding one's life. There is the power of purpose that draws a griever forward through the healing process of grief. That purpose is a combination of exercising the will and resolving to do what is needed to rebuild one's life.

A person can choose to face forward and not always be looking back. While the past informs the present, it is unhealthy do dwell there. Instead, it is a matter of facing the present, and focusing forward. Perhaps it will entail taking baby steps. But choosing to be moving in a direction that will bring healing and wholeness is key to moving forward. A victim will always be focusing on their loss. A survivor will rise each day with certain plans to choose well and become active in refocusing one's life.

It may be the time to struggle with new life patterns. Things are different now. That loved one is no longer present. But his or her life and spirit is an inspiration to keep going, getting better by the day.

People need to be patient with themselves. Rebuilding their lives will take time. There will be setbacks along the way. Such is the ebb and flow of grief. Often it is like two steps forward and one step back. But progress will be made if one persists.

Balance in life is important. This balance is comprised of resting, reading, recreation (including exercise), prayer, and work. All of these things combine to make the adjustments less stressful and a part of the new normal that is emerging.

This is the place where a person begins to take charge of the grief journey and seeks creative means to embrace the loss and utilize what one has learned to build again upon the foundations of a life that has been shaken to its core. Depression may still rear its ugly head, for the first time, or once again. Coping with depres-

> Our grief lives with us long as we live...
> by the very act of weaving our losses
> into that tapestry, we ensure that our
> losses are part of our wholeness.
> —Deborah Morris Coryell,
> *Healing through the Shadow of Loss*

sion is very difficult. Again, determination is needed, as well as friends who understand, and possibly the help of a professional counselor if the depression is deep and long.

THE SPOKE OF FUTURE

Choose to reach out to a new future. While grievers do not want to forget the past or their loved one, there comes a time when a person has to reach out to a new future. This is the point where reconciliation becomes a reality. Rather than completing grief or finishing with it altogether, a person is able to incorporate it into a life that is changed and moving forward.

This is the time of accepting responsibility, successfully managing one's life, regaining confidence and role changing, and setting realistic goals. As people become more future-oriented they regain confidence in their lives. There is reason to celebrate each achievement, each hurdle, each success in moving forward. This gives the survivor a real boost in his/her overall sense of well-being. Gaining a sense of competency in gaining control of one's life enables a person to reach out to others who may need their help.

There is a level of functioning that is most compelling to the survivor and the person around them. A good example is Ned. Ned was several months into his grief following the death of his wife. He had taken care of her for several years, and since she died, he had been like a vessel that had lost its moorings. Ned joined our group, and for a number of meetings, he just seemed to be a distraught victim of grief. But then, something changed. Ned found a young man in his community who needed some work, so the two of them got together and formed a small company. They went around and did small repairs, often for widows. Ned found a new purpose—he was helping other people, and creating meaning and purpose in his life. He had a new awareness of life and had a reason to get up every day.

Persons at this stage are rediscovering the enjoyment of their own company. This is especially relevant for someone who has lost a spouse. While they once thought they couldn't live without their loved one, by now they have become comfortable again in their own skin. There is a stronger sense of autonomy. Grievers are less dependent on others for their emotional stability. They are managing their personal needs in a way that is congruent with the personal goals that they are rediscovering.

A renewed sense of vitality, a level of energy that is compelling, a stability that is admirable—all give evidence of individuals who are well on the road to experiencing healing in their life. Hope is more of a constant and the future is as bright as the promise of God.

CONCLUSION

I was in a small group setting with Elizabeth Neeld. She spoke of the challenges that she had faced in grief and the choices she had to make to survive and love life again. I asked her, given the fact that she had written the classic work *Seven Choices*, if she were to add an eighth choice, what that would be. She responded that she had not been asked that question before, but if she added an eighth choice, it would be "to choose to honor the mystery of life." She qualified this by sharing that life is often so unpredictable, and at some point, one has to be willing to accept the surprising twists and turns that come with life. To do so is to understand that some things cannot be explained, but must be attributed to the mystery of life. Regardless, the wheel of life continues to turn. When the critical yet difficult choices are made in the grief journey, one is put in the position where he or she can move forward with faith and hope for the future.

CHAPTER FIVE

THE IMPORTANCE OF RITUAL

When Job's three friends ... heard about all the troubles that had come upon (Job), they set out from their homes ... then they sat on the ground with him for seven days and nights.
—Job 2:11, 13, NIV

Fresh out of seminary, I was called to be the new assistant minister at a church in the south of England, in the Norman town of Tonbridge, county of Kent. I had never conducted a funeral before and did not have much training in how to do so. Not only was it a different culture, but the main method of body dissolution was by cremation. Early on in my ministry there, the pastor David Beer had gone on holiday (vacation). I was left with all the pastoral responsibilities in his absence. I hoped all would be calm until his return. Little did I know what would happen next. The first Saturday I was on my own, a strange phone call came to my home. An elderly man in a weeping voice on the other end wanted to know if I conducted funerals for dogs. I did not know how to respond, and the pitiful man kept lamenting the loss of his poor dog, and how nobody would help or seemed to care. As he poured out his heart about how much the dog meant to him, I could sense that his grief was overwhelming. I stammered and stuttered with no idea what to do. Just about then, there was silence on the other end. And then I heard a chuckle. Wouldn't you know it was David calling to check on me, and deciding to pull a little prank. Ha ha. Funny. I could have wrung his neck. Still, I breathed a sigh of relief, and joined in the laughter. What a scare I had!

He "rang off," but after a few minutes, the phone rang again. The stately voice at the other end inquired, "Is this the Right Reverend Larry Michael?" Suspecting that this might be another prank, I retorted, "This is he, but I don't know how reverend I am!" Much to my chagrin, the caller introduced himself as Keith Groombridge, the undertaker in the local funeral home. He proceeded to tell me that one of our elderly church members had died, and I had been requested to take the funeral. Needless to say, at that point, I was a bit flabbergasted. But I gathered my wits, made the proper contacts, and met with the family. It turned out okay, but I must admit, I was a bit nervous to push that button during the final prayer at the crematorium, to make the coffin descend downward to the depths below. When people opened their eyes at the end of the prayer, it was magically gone! That was a new experience for me, one of many to come in the following years.

While I encountered many different experiences in my years of pastoral ministry, I am only one of a long procession of ministers who have conducted funerals throughout the ages. For the most part, I and perhaps others tend to consider the contemporary situation in isolation. But, in reality, the funeral has been an important part of ritual since time immemorial. Getting a grip on grief means understanding the importance of ritual in the grieving process.

THE ROLE OF RITUAL

The history of funeral ritual is quite interesting related to the various traditions and customs that have been established in many different cultures. In ancient times, the ritual mostly related to the actual funeral ceremony, a place for the dead to be buried, and a way to memorialize them. Early burial grounds of Neanderthals show that items like animal antlers on the body and remnants of flowers reveal specific rituals of remembrance. Some primitive cultures even placed the body in the depth of the jungle where it was devoured by wild beasts. This practice related to fears of evil spirits and the belief that their loved ones would fare better in another world.

In many cultures, the genders were handled differently at death. The Ghonds buried their women but cremated their men. The Cochlieans buried their women, but hung their men from trees. The Bongas buried their men with their faces to the North and their women with their faces to the South. These are only a few examples of death ritual that may seem strange to us today, but they held specific meaning within their own contexts. Many of the traditions emanated from fear of pagan gods, and were efforts to appease them and lead their loved ones to a safe eternal rest. People of faith view ritual as different, as full of hope in anticipation of an eternal life in heaven for their loved ones. Rather than fear-based for the Christian, there is confidence in "the hope that is steadfast and sure" (Hebrews 6:19).

Mourning ritual took on various expressions in the Bible, beginning with the Hebrews in the Old Testament, as indicated by several examples listed below:

- There is the example of fasting when King Saul and his son Jonathan were killed in battle. 2 Samuel 1:12, ESV—"And they mourned and wept and fasted until evening for Saul and for Jonathan his son and for the people of the LORD and for the house of Israel, because they had fallen by the sword."

- A period of mourning was designated by the Hebrews after Aaron the priest died. Numbers 20:29, ESV—"And when all the congregation saw that Aaron had perished, all the house of Israel wept for Aaron thirty days."

- When the patriarch Jacob died, his son Joseph (second in command after Pharaoh in Egypt) had him embalmed. Genesis 50:1–3, ESV—"Then Joseph fell on his father's face and wept over him and kissed him. And Joseph commanded his servants the physicians to embalm his father. So the physicians embalmed Israel. Forty days were required for it, for that is how many are required for embalming. And the Egyptians wept for him seventy days."

- Professional mourners were assigned a specific role when someone died. Jeremiah 9:17, ESV—"Thus says the LORD of hosts: 'Consider, and call for the mourning women to come; send for the skillful women to come.'"

- The rending of clothes with sackcloth and ashes was a common ritual when someone died in the Old Testament, as recorded when David's son Absalom died. 2 Samuel 3:31, ESV—"Then

David said to Joab and to all the people who were with him, 'Tear your clothes and put on sackcloth and mourn before Abner.' And King David followed the bier."

Biblical accounts demonstrate the importance of ceremonial ritual when a person died. The precedent has come down to contemporary times, albeit with some variation.

Rituals give us the opportunity to engage in activities that provide substance and meaning in our lives. Kenneth Doka provides useful information about the essential role ritual plays in relation to a person's grief experience. For example, a man cooks his deceased wife's favorite meal on her birthday. While no one else benefits from the meal, for him it is a celebration of her life on her special day for him to enjoy alone. It is ritual. It has special meaning.

There are four functions of ritual that Doka elucidates in a variety of situations:

- Rituals of Continuity—This type of ritual implies that the person is still part of my life and there exists a continuing bond. The birthday ritual described above is an example of this.

- Rituals of Transition—This marks that a change has taken place in the grief response. For example, parents who have lost a child marked a transition in their mourning by cleaning out their deceased child's room after a period of time acceptable to them.

- Rituals of Affirmation—This is a ritual act whereby one writes a letter or poem to the deceased thanking the person for the caring, love, help, and support. This is especially useful for those who never had the opportunity to say "thank you."

- Rituals of Intensification—This type of ritual intensifies connection among group members and reinforces their common identity—for example, the AIDS Quilt, the Vietnam War Memorial, the Oklahoma City Memorial Park.[1]

---

1. Kenneth J. Doka, ed., *Disenfranchised Grief: New Directions, Challenges, and Strategies for Practice* (Champaign, IL: Research Press, 2002).

THE IMPORTANCE OF THE FUNERAL

The funeral or memorial service is an important part of the ritual related to death. I am among those who believe that the funeral is a functional part of the grieving process that should not be devalued. While there are movements today away from ritualistic ways of paying tribute to a person's life, the traditional methods provide authentic ways for people to express grief as well as celebrate all that the person meant to them.

The importance of the funeral ritual cannot be overemphasized. People in all nations utilize ceremonies to memorialize their loved ones in ways that reflect their understanding about death. Funerals serve the purpose of not only remembering that the person has died, but brings significant tribute to the life that was lived. Typically, they are public services that include not only family, but friends, neighbors, and other acquaintances. They offer survivors the opportunity to gather and share the events and remembrances of the person's life. The funeral provides a place for loved ones to express their feelings, speak about the deceased, share special memories, and pay their respects to all that the person meant to them. In addition, family and other mourners are enabled to embrace their faith and seek hope that will enable them to carry on in the person's absence.

The funeral is a stark reminder that a death has occurred, and that reality is a necessary part of grief. For Christians, the funeral has further meaning and expresses faith in the promise of the resurrection to eternal life. Jesus recognized the importance of the funeral ritual. While at the same time, it has been said that Jesus never officiated at a funeral, he only officiated at resurrections! On several occasions when Jesus arrived at a death scene, he respected what was going on and shared in the mourning. His presence was an acknowledgement of the grief ritual that was occurring. The difference was that he transformed each situation from the pall of death to the celebration of life.

Alan Wolfelt, in his book *Understanding Your Grief: Ten Essential Touchstones for Finding Hope and Healing Your Heart,* expounds the importance of the funeral ritual based on a *hierarchy of purpose*. He identifies six different factors that elucidate its role: ***Transcendence***, in which funerals help us embrace the wonder of life and death; ***Meaning***, in which funerals mark the significance of the life that was lived, and further provide us with meaning and purpose in our continued living; ***Expression***, in which funerals allow us to express our inner thoughts and feelings about life and death; **Support**, whereupon funerals bring together a collective group who care for one another in a secure atmosphere that promotes love and support; **Recall**, whereupon funerals encourage us to remember the person who died and share our unique memories of that person with others; and **Reality**, in which funerals help us begin to truly acknowledge the reality that someone in our life has died.

THE CHANGING NATURE OF FUNERALS

Funerals traditionally have focused on grieving the person's death, but in more recent years the focus has shifted to a celebration of the loved one's life. This perhaps is evident in the shift from funeral with body followed by burial, to the practice today of private burial followed by memorial service without the body. I remember the first time I experienced this while serving a pastorate in Kentucky. It was the memorial service the Rev. Beer, whom we were introduced to at the beginning of this chapter. His family decided to have a private burial before the service. It seemed strange then, some twenty years ago, but now has become a more common order of observance.

Funerals have not only experienced a transformation in the United States but in other countries as well. When Rev. Beer died, his committal at the crematorium occurred firstly with family and special friends, then we proceeded to the church for a wonderful memorial service.

Nevertheless, funeral rites and observances vary according to local culture. As time passes, funeral customs will no doubt continue to morph and evolve as they have to this point. Certainly prominent at Christian funerals is the belief and awareness that this loved one has been promoted to heaven to receive their eternal reward. It is a real sense of celebration that this

> I have wept at funerals, and yet also shared in this sense of something like triumph. A good and well-loved life has ended, and that is sad. But that same life is now transformed into a new and better existence, by the power of God, and that is a glorious triumph.
> —David Winter, *Living through Loss*

person is now free from pain, suffering, and liberated from all the trials on earth. But the funeral is also a place to recognize the overwhelming sense of loss this side of heaven. Doug Manning gives a wonderful treatment to the changing nature of funerals in his book *The Funeral*.

In recent years, there has been a reduction in traditional funeral services. Some people question the necessity of a funeral and are choosing to have no service whatsoever. They think that the funeral makes it harder on the family, and it would be easier to avoid it altogether. So they decide that they want to throw a party at someone's house rather than have a somber service. Others may have no observance at all, or just say a few words at the graveside.

The traditional funeral has often been preceded by an open-casket in the United States (in England this is viewed as morbid, and only the family views the body privately in a small parlor). While this tradition varies today, many grief experts advocate that viewing the body helps family and others to accept the reality of the death. I remember how this affected me personally as a young minister—when I was on a summer mission experience in England. Upon my arrival there, I learned of my grandfather's death back in Maryland. It was impossible for me to return for the funeral, and for a long time his passing seemed mysterious and unresolved. It helped so much when my Uncle Richard Springer saved my grandfather's ring for me, made from a black onyx stone that my uncle had brought back from Italy while serving in the Navy. It was a most generous gesture that has been a treasured keepsake for me all these years. I wear that ring today, and remember well the love I shared and still have for my grandfather.

All of this is to say that the finality of death is striking when one sees

> The death of a loved one is not a normal everyday event, and the confusion that often surrounds the death is not a normal, everyday kind of confusion. It's bigger than that. It can be strange. It can be disturbing, and sometimes it can be mystifying. Death pulls at the veil of mundane life and, at least temporarily, exposes us to a universe of questions, many of which have no clear answer.
>
> —George A. Bonano,
> *The Other Side of Sadness*

the person lying there. Mourners may view the death as real on an intellectual level, but it is important that they also accept its reality on an emotional level. Viewing a body emotes a response that acknowledges that this person is not coming back. Alan Wolfelt reminds us that we have to say goodbye to the person before we can say hello to our grief (For more information on funeral planning see Appendix II—Funeral Planning Checklist).

WHEN DEATH OCCURS

The timing of a death is mostly unpredictable. When a leader is called to a family who has lost a loved one, it no doubt will be a most trying situation. They will encounter a family that is distraught and looking for comfort and direction. But it is a valuable time when their presence can offer tremendous help to loved ones as they deal with their loss and begin to think about preparations for a funeral or memorial service. A leader is well-served to have given some thought to a plan, leading a family through necessary steps in providing a service that is meaningful and pays respect to their loved one.

There are some helpful rules that apply when this first visit with the family occurs. Leaders need to be as prompt as possible in getting there. They will seek to be helpful in every way they can. And, they do not overextend their time with the family—unless they are asked to stay for a while. A leader will make proper expressions of sympathy and engage in appropriate discussion about the death and help the grievers to cope with the immediate situation at hand in their grief.

Quite a few times in my ministry I was present with the family when their loved one died. So in a real sense the first meeting had already happened. What I did in those situations when appropriate was to join hands with the family, offer a prayer, thanking God for the person's life and all that the person meant to us, affirmed that God loved them more than we ever could, asked for peace and comfort for the family, prayed that they would be strengthened in the days to come, and committing them to the Lord's keeping. Sometimes, it seemed apt to sing a verse of a favorite hymn together and sometimes it did not. (Being able to carry a tune is important in this regard.)

This is not the time simply to trot out well-worn phrases about death— "They're in a better place," "God has taken them home"—in a perfunctory manner. While a leader may fall back on playing the professional role and offering truisms, it is best to come alongside them in an authentic way like that favorite doctor who would display empathy at a patient's bedside. Comforting them, communicating that he/she will be there for them, praying with them, and spending quality time at a time of crisis, will show a family that there is real care and concern.

If a leader is not present when the death occurs, usually the first person to be informed is a funeral director. The family typically then begin to use their phones to inform other family members. According to the relationship that the leader may have with the person's family, the leader may be the next one to know, depending on how many immediate family members may need to be contacted before the leader is contacted. It would be useful for the leader to find ways to remind the congregation that the pastor should be contacted as soon as possible. This could be incorporated into a regular newsletter, etc. Leaders should know that death is never convenient. Sometimes, the phone will ring on their day off. That does not mean they should not go. They should. It's their role. They belong there. Ministry is not a work of convenience but a calling that comes at any time.

> People don't care how much you know until they know how much you care.
> —John Maxwell

On the occasions when I was informed of a member or loved one's death, I then went to the home or hospital or nursing home as soon as possible. If I went to the home, then I usually did the following: Upon entering the home, I often hugged family members, expressed how sorry I was to hear of their loved one passing, and then we usually sat down and I let them talk about the passing of their loved one according to the comfort level of the family. After offering condolences, listening to the loved ones tell their story, then basic information is gathered, and a follow-up visit is arranged—that could occur at the church, at the family's home, or even sometimes with the family at the funeral home.

FOLLOW-UP MEETING WITH THE FAMILY

At the planning meeting with family members, they will want to recount fond remembrances of the deceased, favorite stories, Scripture that was meaningful to them, readings/poetry, music for the service, family traditions, length of service, others to be involved in the service, eulogies to be offered by family members or friends, memorials, flowers, photo displays, and a fellowship meal for the family and friends.

Sometimes, the family may make requests that seem unconventional. My rule of thumb was always to allow the family to personalize the service as long as it did not interfere with the rules of decorum that I deemed appropriate for a Christian service. I had one pastor from England tell me if he had one more request for "My Way" to be played that he would throw up. That might seem a bit extreme, but in leadership we must remember that the main thrust is to honor God and pay tribute to the person in an appropriate manner.

During the visit, the leader will want to obtain some basic information. Some of the important questions one might ask are the following:

- Where will the service be conducted (funeral home, church, chapel, cemetery, etc.)?
- What day and time for the service? (in consultation with the funeral director)
- Will the service be public or private?
- Is there any other minister to be involved in the service?
- Will there be any other rites to occur (military, etc.)?
- Will there be any music? Hymns? Solos?
- Family involvement (eulogy, readings, etc)?
- Did the deceased leave any personal instructions?
- Favorite Scripture text?
- A formal obituary, to be read?
- Where will the final resting place be?
- Is there anything else we can do to help? (contact persons, etc.)?
- What about food after the funeral? (church provided, etc.)
- Do you have any special requests for the service?

ASSISTING IN NECESSARY RESPONSIBILITIES

A leader is in a position to make referrals in assisting a family to initiate responsibilities for the person's estate. This would include helping with necessary items and responsibilities that need to be taken care of, especially if it is a widow/widower. Law requires a certain number of death certificates for various legal items. Widows are very vulnerable and it would be useful for the leader to know some of the items they may need.

Leaders could refer the survivors to a financial planner if they don't already have one. This would help greatly in dealing with financial obligations and planning for the future, establishing a budget, etc. Sometimes, people will make poor financial decisions in their time of grieving. Sufficient counsel might help them avoid expenditures that could be costly long-term.

Many people are not always informed regarding necessary steps they need to take regarding legal issues, etc. As well, they are often confused and bewildered and unable to make certain decisions early on. It may be appropriate to refer grievers to a lawyer, if they don't already have one. This would help in estate matters.

The leader may be consulted about funeral services, but unless the death is sudden, many people have already given some thought to what funeral home they want to use. And yet there are many who do not make these decisions, but leave them to the family. If one is asked, counsel may be given to help families make selections that will not be way above their budget. I have actually gone to funeral homes with families to help them make arrangements. My presence counted in the sense that the funeral director did not try to oversell the family. As well, it was a source of comfort to have me there, as they sometimes were indecisive and would ask my opinion.

PLANNING THE FUNERAL OR MEMORIAL SERVICE

The variations of a funeral service are many. Typically, the order includes a welcome, reading Scripture, prayer, hymns, reading the obituary, special music, brief eulogy by family or friend, main Scripture, message/sermon, hymn, benediction. Reading an obituary is a common practice in some parts of the country. While it may be sentimentally written and contain information that is superfluous, most ministers or officiants will concede to include it in the body of the service. It does bring acknowledgement to the survivors, family associations of the deceased, and provides useful information to attendees who did not know the deceased (For more information on appropriate scripture for funerals, see Appendix III—Grief and the Scriptures).

Some services may include communion, affirmation of faith, the Lord's Prayer, the Twenty-Third Psalm, poetry, etc. In the past, instructions had been given regarding directions to the cemetery, where a brief committal service occurred. Typically, services I conducted there were very brief, and included only a Scripture reading (often 1 Thessalonians 4:13–18), and a prayer of committal. If there is only a graveside service, then the typical funeral service can be abbreviated with a brief message, and include the prayer of committal with benediction.

One source of irritation for me occurred when family members stated that they wanted the service to be very brief, not more than five to ten minutes. I gulped. They said it would be difficult for the family, and they didn't want to prolong it. Well, grief is difficult. But a funeral is a time when people should be given the chance to pay appropriate tribute to a person's life, and give people the opportunity to express their remembrances of the person. Still, as much as possible, it is helpful to accommodate family wishes.

> The heart of grief, its most difficult challenge, is not "letting go" of those who have died but instead making the transition from loving in presence to loving in separation.
> —Thomas Attig,
> *The Heart of Grief: Death and the Search for Lasting Love*

VARIABLES IN THE FUNERAL SERVICE

Today, occurring more frequently, there is a memorial service without the presence of the body. Many families are choosing to do this after the cremation or private burial, when they then can celebrate the person's life and have a meaningful worship experience.

If the body is present in the service, complete with casket, etc., then a decision is made, depending on local culture, whether the casket is to be open or closed. In some places I have served, they left the casket open during the service; mourners proceeded by the casket at the conclusion, and the minister stood at the head of the casket. The last ones to come by were the family, who gathered there for a few minutes to say their farewells, hug one another, shed some tears, and perhaps touch the body.

One never knows as a minister what might happen as a funeral. Even humorous things can happen. One friend told me about his father officiating at a funeral in Kentucky, where people processed by the casket at the end of the service. His father was standing there at the head of the casket, and as people came by, one lady's underwear fell off her legs onto the floor. He said she just stepped out of them, picked them up, and kept moving. He was wanting to laugh, but couldn't. He said after he got in the car, he had to let it out, and laughed for miles driving down the road! That was not disrespectful. It was a needed release for a very tense day.

I am inclined to think that it is a means to dealing with the reality of the loss by viewing the body. Some others believe it is morbid and should only occur in a private setting. This depends on the wishes of the family and what is accepted as a norm in the locale of the service.

I prefer the casket to be closed during the service, because then the focus is not only on the loved one, but also a focus on God and helping with the worship experience.

THE DAY OF THE FUNERAL

The day of the funeral is one of many emotions and consternation for the family. Often they are confused, emotional, and indecisive. Here a leader can be most helpful. It is important to arrive at the place of the service well ahead of the family. The minister wants to be there when loved ones arrive, and assist them in whatever way they can. Having a quiet time with them and praying with them before others arrive can be comforting to them.

If there is visitation right before the funeral, then the same rule applies. Whereas there used to be several days of visitation, more recently, the visitation has been combined with the funeral following shortly thereafter. This allows people to comingle with the family and one another before the formal service begins.

The Graveside Service

"The idea is to send everyone home thinking about life instead of death, and the joys of heaven rather than the desolateness of earth."[2]

One time I attended a graveside service led by another minister, and the day was unusually hot, even for summer. With everyone sweltering in the heat, the service dragged on for what seemed an incessantly long

---

2. Andrew Watterson Blackwood, *The Funeral: A Source Book for Ministers* (Philadelphia: Westminster Press, 1942), 151.

period of time. One elderly retired pastor standing next to me, who was stone deaf, remarked in a rather loud voice, "He just doesn't know what he's doing, does he?" There were side glances toward us, and I was somewhat embarrassed, but the saintly old minister spoke the truth. Graveside services should be brief unless there are extenuating circumstances, and kept to a maximum of fifteen to twenty minutes. In my experience, typically people do not linger for long periods of time in the cemetery, but it is important to let the immediate family take the lead. It may be an important time to exchange final condolences before departure and interment.

> God shall wipe all tears from their eyes; and there shall be no more death, nor crying, neither shall there be any more pain: for the former things are passed away.
> —Revelation 21:4

Difficult Circumstances

I remember having to take a most difficult funeral of a young man who was stabbed to death. I knew little about him or his life, but tried to make the most of the situation for the family. The best I could do, given the circumstances, was to speak on Psalm 103, the love of God. It is perhaps one of the most meaningful texts to use when one does not know much about the person or their spiritual situation.

There are often difficulties related to mixed family situations at funerals. I remember once in Indiana when I was conducting a service that I realized at the end that there were two families present. The funeral director had a curtain that separated the two families. So, when the service was concluded, they filed by the casket, the former wife and children. And then, at the last the curtain was opened, and the current wife and family filed by. It was most difficult, and you could cut the tension in the air with a knife. Funerals bring out the best and the worst when it comes to family situations. Unfortunately, some folks are already focused on the will and what will be left to them. This leads to squabbles and worse.

A most difficult circumstance occurred in a church where a staff member died of a heart attack while in bed with a church member. The staff and leadership of the church covenanted to keep the circumstances of the death to themselves in order to protect the privacy of the widow. They were able to minister to the staff member's family, conducted a memorial service at the church, arranged for the body to be transitioned to the home state for burial, and kept the emotional disturbance and upheaval at the church to a minimum.

Let's not forget the secondary losses that are precipitated by the death of a loved one. These exacerbate the situation and make it more difficult. For some survivors there may be the loss of financial security, a home, independence, status in the community, changes in friendships, etc. For those who lose a child, they have lost an important role as a parent. For some others the secondary losses could be abstract in the sense of all their hopes and dreams for the future that have been shattered by the death of a loved one.

As well, there are those losses that are not socially recognized, as with someone having an affair, someone suffering a miscarriage, losing a pet, etc. This type of loss is termed a "disenfranchised loss," and usually refers to that which others may believe is not a legitimate loss. Grief is grief regardless. And, don't dare tell that expectant mother who was carrying a child within her that her loss was not a real loss. There is great grief that occurs when a couple loses an unborn child.

The Burial or Final Disposition

Significant and powerful is the manner in what is termed as "the final disposition." It is a time of crisis for some, having to commit their loved one to a final place. But the moment when someone is laid to rest is a significant transition for a grieving family. In essence, they are saying goodbye to the person and hello to their grief. It is not a time of closure, but a time to physically let go of the person and contemplate a changed life.

The choices are numerous. There is burial in the ground. There is above-ground entombment. There is cremation. It may include embalming and visitation. Or the cremation can be done immediately. The cost is much less when cremation is used. Some people scatter the ashes, some bury them, and some place them an urn or appropriate container. Still, there are churches that provide columbariums for the final resting places of church members. These are usually located in gardens or a place of solace on the church grounds.

Cremation was somewhat taboo in the United States fifty years ago, but as recently as 2011, indications were that cremation is now chosen over burial in forty-one percent of American deaths, according to the

Cremation Association of North America. Much of this increase of fifteen percent from 1985 is due to economic factors, cremation being much more affordable than a traditional funeral.

CONCLUSION

As a leader, one will be called upon on many occasions to officiate or assist in a funeral or memorial service. It is one of the highest privileges of ministry, to offer solace and comfort to those who have lost a dear loved one. It calls for preparation, spiritually and practically, to bring one's best efforts to each situation. As leaders seek to bring the comfort of God to each family, they will be led by God's Spirit to touch each life with their presence, their word, their prayers, and their compassion. One should never underestimate the importance of the funeral, and the lasting impact it will have on those who have been left behind. They may not remember all of one's words, but they will never forget the love and care shown to them in their time of need.

CHAPTER SIX

MINISTERING TO SPECIFIC LOSSES

Jesus wept.
—John 11:35, ESV

Every loss of a loved one is significant, though it may be necessary to delineate the different impact that specific losses can have on a person's life. Whether the loss is a parent, child, spouse, grandparent, sibling, friend, or others close to you, it merits a level of understanding and attention. Too often in the frantic-paced world in which we live, losses can be overlooked or underestimated, even by those who are close to a survivor. Leaders can be aware and alert to distinctions of different losses and respond accordingly. That is the reason for this chapter, giving a heads-up on various ways these loved ones are hurting and how they may be helped. This can be an exhaustive topic, and for the purposes of this work, a brief treatment will be given for each loss. There are many books and articles that have dealt with these losses, and I would encourage leaders to seek them out for additional guidance.

A factor that is well to be remembered is the reality of *differential loss* in a family. It is the situation after a loved one dies where family members grieve in unique ways, at different paces, with varying intensity, which can bring a strain on the family unit with accompanying conflict. An example of this is a widow who shared that her children did not understand the depth of her grief for her husband and told her to stop crying. They loved their dad but their grief was different. Their lack of understanding was so hurtful to her. Thankfully, she got into a grief support group and was able to get support from others who had experienced the same loss as she had experienced. Another example was a husband and wife who came to a session where I spoke on the fallacies of grief. Their young adult son had died two years before, and they were at very different places in the grief process. He shared that he had come to a place of acceptance and peace, whereas his wife was still actively grieving, visiting her son's graveside every day and was stuck in a continual state of sadness. Their situation is not dissimilar from other couples who have lost a child. The differing grief often creates conflict in the relationship.

> It is as if each family were a huge ball of yarn; each member a different colored strand woven and wound together. When one member dies, the entire ball must be unwound, the strand removed, and the ball then needs to be put back together and rewound. However, the ball can never be recreated as it was before.
>
> —Jean Galica

DIFFERING LOSSES

Loss of a Spouse

Many of the grief support groups I lead involve survivors who have lost a spouse. While every death of a loved one is life changing in some manner, those who have lost their mate often say it is the most traumatic loss in their life. They feel like they have been cut in half, and their heart has been severed in two. The term "emotional earthquake" is a relevant one in this situation. The plans they had for the future have been shattered, with all hopes and dreams dashed in the process. They often have such intense emotions because of the close intimate nature of the relationship. Even their own families don't understand the severity of their grief.

Spouses tend to feel a lot of guilt, especially in regard to the future, and being able to move on with their lives. A friend of the family called one lady two years after her husband died, and he recounted how she was still fretful about making any decision that her husband would have disapproved. Sometimes the grief is not over the loss of a great relationship.

If the relationship had major issues and problems, there is grief over un-resolved issues and what "might have been."

A number of spouses I have encountered who were caregivers also experienced guilt. A lot of that guilt came from the fact that they felt a sense of relief and freedom after such a long time of responsibility with their partner. As well, they often blamed themselves for the things they were unable to do to bring relief at the end.

Author C. S. Lewis kept a personal journal after losing his wife Joy, focusing on the grief he experienced. He took that journal and used it as a basis for the much acclaimed book, *A Grief Observed*. His insights have proved helpful to many spouses who have experienced the heartache of losing their mate.

Some of the things that spouses may feel:
- An overwhelming sense of loneliness.
- The feeling that their life is over since their mate is gone.
- The belief that they have lost their security.
- A sensation of memory that their loved one is close by.
- Frightened about the future.
- Insecure about doing duties done by their spouse.
- A mountain of responsibility in handling legal and financial matters.
- Survivor's guilt that they should have been taken instead.
- Anger that their spouse left them.
- Hopelessness about unfulfilled plans and dreams.
- Hate to eat at restaurants alone.
- Feel out of place with couples.

Some of the coping strategies for encouraging spouses might include:
- Let others help them who offer to do so.
- Share about their partners and their memories.
- Plan and set limits regarding holidays and difficult anniversaries.
- Don't make major decisions during the first year if possible.
- Benefit from participating in a grief support group with others who have lost spouses.
- Honor the memory of their partners in appropriate ways to include other family.
- Receive permission to take steps to re-direct their lives.
- Take their time in dealing with personal items of their spouse.

Loss of a Child

Every year close to 60,000 children (ages one to twenty-four) die in America.[1] Almost half of those deaths are infant deaths. Beyond the age of twenty-four, the deaths of adult children bring the total closer to 300,000 per year. Needless to say, the loss of a child, regardless of the age, is one of the hardest losses a family can experience. Parents lament the reversal of the order of life, saying that it's not right that their child should die before they do. They expect their children to outlive them. As a result, families are left reeling, struggling to cope with an inestimable tragedy. I have ministered to families who have just suffered the loss of a newborn, a teenage girl killed in a car accident, a young man suffering a heart attack on the basketball court, adult children who have died with cancer, to name some of the varied child loss situations. Regardless of the age, losing a child is one of the saddest experiences one can imagine. While not an enviable situation for any leader, it does provide an opportunity to bring a healing presence to a family whose lives have forever been changed because an untimely death has taken one of their own.

John Claypool was a veteran pastor who had served churches for close to twenty years when he encountered a most severe challenge to his life and ministry. His eight-year-old daughter, Laura Lue, was diagnosed with acute leukemia, and after only eighteen months died from her illness. Reflecting on this experience as her father, John wrote *Tracks of a Fellow Struggler,* a book based on

> She asked me in the dark of the night: "When will this leukemia go away?" I answered: "I don't know, darling, but we are doing everything we know to make that happen." Then she said: "Have you asked God when it will go away?" And I said: "Yes, you have heard me pray to him many times." But she persisted: "What did God say? When did God say it would go away?" And I had to admit God had not said a word! I had done a lot of talking and praying and pleading, but the response of the heavens had been one of silence.
>
> —John Claypool

---

1. http://www.cdc.gov/nchs/data/nvsr/nvsr61/nvsr61_06.pdf; accessed October 30, 2014.

four sermons he shared with his congregation after Laura Lue's death. In the preface, John wrote: "This little book reflects my own encounter with the realities of terminal illness and the death and the grief that follows. It is written from the inside of events, not the outside." His honest insights based on the experience of grief's effect on his faith have helped many people since that time. The Bible tells us that God is no respecter of persons. Even pastors are not exempt from the tragedy of losing a child.

The death of a child brings great strain upon the family unit, especially to the marriage of the parents. The husband and wife often find it difficult to help one another because of their individual responses to handling grief which may be different. While there are marriages that end in divorce as a result, it is not as prevalent as many would think.[2] What is needed are caring individuals who will reach out to the couple and provide support during what will be a prolonged grief process. Patient understanding of the ramifications of the loss of a child are necessary for leaders to come to terms with the extent of the loss to a family. The hopes and dreams that the parents had for the child, the loss of parenting, their self-identity, and much more are changed forever because their child has died.

Ways that parents cope include a number of things. Many of the ways already discussed in this book are applicable. But beyond that, parents may honor and remember their child in specific ways. Create a lasting memory of the child, such as making scrapbooks, penning a history of the child, establishing a scholarship in the child's name, are all special ways to memorialize. My brother and sister-in-law created a scholarship in memory of their son Jimmy at the college he had attended. It is a meaningful way to extend his memory in the community.

Leaders should be careful not to overlook the parents who have suffered a miscarriage. While the child may not have come to full term, it was a living being that the mother carried within her for a distinct period of time. The grief may be immense for this loss. Even more, stillbirths are especially difficult, and for some mothers, they have known beforehand and have had to carry a deceased child to term. I have conducted funerals for stillborn infants, and my heart went out to those parents who had

---

2. Cited at http://jfs.e-contentmanagement.com/archives/vol/4/issue/2/article/2513/the-impact-of-a-childs-death-on-parents; accessed October 30, 2014, based on article by R. Schwab, "Effects of a child's death on the marital relationship: A preliminary study," *Death Studies*, 14, 407–422 (1992).

placed such hope and longing for this child that was now taken from them. A great degree of sensitivity and compassion is needed for this situation. They are grieving their loss and also grieving what might have been.

Loss of an Adult Child

Losing a child who is an adult is very painful for the parents. Again, it is a reversal of the natural order in that the parents expected their child to outlive them. In a parent's loss of an adult child, much of the focus and attention will be upon the child's family. If they were married, and had their own children, their parents can be overlooked. As well, if the adult child was single, then there are legal issues related to finance, property, and will with which the parents must contend. Often, the parents will have to reach out to their grandchildren and in-laws. Leaders will do well to recognize the needs that parents have, even though they may be up in years. I knew a couple who took in their son into their home in his final days, even though they were in their eighties. It was a difficult time for them, but they provided the care he needed, and adjusted their lives to provide for him in his final days. They liked to talk about him and remember all the ways in which he touched their lives, as well as the lives of others. Leaders do well not to overlook the parents in this type of adult child loss.

Grieving parents often have a desire to do something positive and lasting in memory of their sons or daughters. Many have established memorial funds, created scholarships, made donations to special charities, given books to libraries, given commemorative gifts, planted trees, and become involved in service to others through their church or other organizations. For many, such acts help to keep the memories of their children alive and vibrant, giving them and others opportunities to feel the beauty of the life and love of their child. Not only are these activities a wonderful tribute, but they can also be a means to healing while providing a sense of purpose to the parent.

Adult Loss of a Parent

The loss of a parent is the single most common loss for an adult.[3] Losing a parent as an adult is tougher than some people may think. I lost my

---

3. Therese A. Rando, "Adult Loss of a Parent," excerpt from *How to Go On Living When Someone You Love Dies* (New York: Bantam Books). Cited by http://www.trucare.org/sites/default/files/pdfs/grief-and-loss/parent-loss/adult-loss-of-a-parent.pdf; accessed October 30, 2014.

> No one knows you in the exact same way as your mother or father— indeed, will *ever* know you as your parent did.
> —Therese Rando

mother in 2013, and though she was eighty-nine years old, I miss her tremendously. Yes, she lived to a ripe old age, but she was my mom. And this side of heaven, I will not see her again. She won't be there to hug me, tell me she loves me, and that she is proud of me. And, I also miss her prayers.

Losing one parent is difficult enough, but when you lose the second parent, there is a finality that a significant part of your life is gone. It shifts the generational responsibility from them to you, and the reality now that you are the parent, and one day your children will face the same loss. It is all part of the cycle of life, and adjustments must be made accordingly.

"The death of a parent can certainly be a life-changing event for an adult child, especially those who have been serving as caregivers." So says Joan, a woman in the grief support group at our church, who went on to share more about her experience with grief:

> My 88-year-old mother's three-year experience with dementia and three-day dying process as her body closed down left me with panic attacks and fear that I was losing my mind. I became afraid my husband would die and leave me too. Feeling isolated, lonely and drained of energy after three years of being a caregiver, I joined a grief support group and learned that this is a normal part of grief. The panic attacks subsided as I was able to talk about my experience with my new friends in the group. Now I am beginning to enjoy life once again with the assurance that Mom will always live in my heart.
>
> —Joan Scott Lowe

Leaders should be cognizant of the tremendous loss felt by adults who have cared for aging parents that have died. Especially if they were single, lived with that parent, and offered continual care on a daily basis, the impact will be much greater and need care and consideration.

AGE-RELATED GRIEVERS

Helping Children Grieve

At some point every child must learn about death. Years ago such knowledge was a part of life at a younger age as children were exposed more to death than today. As child mortality has decreased in recent years, and family members are living longer, children may not encounter a family death until their teens or even older. But it will happen. They may experience the loss of a grandparent, a friend, a sibling, or a parent. According to the US Census Bureau, one in twenty children under the age of eighteen will experience the death of a parent. The loss of a parent turns a child's world upside down. A woman in one of our grief support groups had small children who discovered their young father dead in the shower of a heart attack. It was indeed a terrible shock, and one for which they and their mother were unprepared. Adults needs to understand that death does have a great impact on children. They are smarter than some adults think, and they think a lot about things—both the beginnings and the end of life. So, it is necessary to be sensitive to what children are experiencing, and not overlook their grief.

When I was a very small child I coped with death in a way that I later discovered was not unusual. I diverted my grief by thinking that those who died were just born as someone else. That was a great comfort to me. But, then, as I learned more about faith and death, I came to understand that persons I loved who died had transitioned to a new and better existence called heaven. That helped a great deal, even though I was very sad and missing them.

Children have specific needs when they experience loss. Oftentimes they are overlooked, people mistakenly thinking that children will adjust well and are flexible in their response to life changes. It is important to talk to children. Let them express their feelings. Sometimes, the use of drawings, or toys, puppets, etc. can help them to tell you what they are thinking and feeling. They could be asked to draw a picture of their loved one or friend and where they believe they are now. And, telling them to draw a picture of themselves will give you a clue as to their state of mind. The colors they use may represent feelings of sadness, loneliness, anger, etc. Children are often more open and natural in their grief responses than adults tend to be.

Children can be encouraged with physical outlets like games and sports. While they may express anger, it does not excuse bad behavior. Perhaps, say "I understand that you are angry about grandpa dying. We are all feeling bad, but your behavior is not acceptable. We need to talk about what is going on with you at this time."

Don't answer any more than they ask at that moment. The tendency for adults is to give more information than the child really requires. Be truthful but sensitive to the extent of details they need to know in regard to the death of their loved one (For more information on age-related grieving see Appendix I—Different Ages Grieve in Different Ways).

QUESTIONS CHILDREN MIGHT ASK

Children will ask all kinds of questions. Remember, there are no perfect answers. The best tack is to be patient, and answer the questions to help children understand at their level.

Q: What does "dead" mean?
A: Dead means people stop breathing and their bodies don't work anymore.

Q: Was grandma hurting when she died?
A: She had medicine that helped her not to hurt.

Q: Where is daddy now?
A: He is in heaven and some day we will see him again. (Ask the child what they think about heaven.)

Q. What is Bobby doing in heaven now? (brother)
A: We don't know exactly what he is doing, but we believe he is there with lots of other people and very happy.

Q. Why did mommy have to die?
A: We don't know exactly why she had to die, but she is still present in our hearts.

Q: Was it my fault that sissy died?
A: No, none of us did anything to make this happen.

Q: Why did grandpa die?
A: He got sick and his body could not get better.

While sharing with children, the most helpful message to them is that their loved one is no longer suffering, in pain, sad, sick, and is now in a place where they are happy and whole. That is the blessing of the Christian message. When I was a child that was the most comforting thought of all. I certainly missed my grandparents and others in my family who died. But, I continually reminded myself that they were in a state of blissful contentment in heaven.

If children are upset and even upset with God, know that how you respond is important to their understanding. You can be a positive model to them in various ways: Let them know that you trust God regardless of what has happened; share positive ways that God has helped you in your life; help them to remember that God was there before this happened and will still be there for them; be real with them and express appropriate feelings, encouraging them to do the same.

Children need to know it is safe to express their emotions. Get them to talk about the person, and share their thoughts and questions. If there is trauma with excessive bouts of anger or depression, it may be wise to consult with a professional counselor. Support from family therapists who specialize in grief counseling can be most helpful. There are also specialized counseling centers that have programs for grieving children.

Teens Responding to Loss[4]

Teenagers are sometimes overlooked by adults when someone close to them dies. How they respond to the death of a parent, a grandparent, sibling, a friend may be different than adults respond. They are not children, yet they are not adults. Because of their challenging life phases, they have their own grief issues that may be unique to their age and relationships. Leaders need to be aware of some of those behaviors when seeking to help them. They do experience most of the emotions of grief like many other people do when they lose a loved one, but there are some particular characteristics of their grieving process that are important to note.

---

4. Adapted from "Teens & Grief," Donna Schuurman, Ed.D. & Amy Barrett Lindholm, M.S., *The Prevention Researcher*, Volume 9, Number 2, 2002, Pages 1, 3–5.

The grieving process can leave teens feeling alone and isolated. They may experience withdrawal from social situations. Some teens may go to the other extreme and become hyperactive. They may have mood swings and some regressive/aggressive behavior. There may be a decline in grades because of lack of concentration. All of these symptoms may be normal during grief.

The Death of a Friend—Peer relationships are very important to teens, sometimes more important than family relationship. When they lose a close friend, it can shatter their world. Perhaps for the first time they are confronting death with someone their own age. It may affect their relationship with other surviving peers. They may come together and share their grief, or they may be embarrassed to talk about it and turn inward with their thoughts and feelings.

The Death of a Parent—Naturally, one would expect the death of a parent to have a major impact on a teenager. It is a life-changing event in many ways, affecting their relationship to their family, their security is threatened, their life becomes defined by their loss, and they sense that things will never be the same again. They may have to take on new responsibility, realized a shifting of family roles, fear the lack of financial stability, worry about their plans for the future. Depending on the relationship to the parent, there may be

> Telling the truth and giving choices will assist grieving teens to regain a sense of control of their lives.
> – Donna Schuurmann

mixed emotions if it was strained—guilt, regret, or perhaps relief. They may fret over whether something will happen to them or the surviving parent.

Death of a Sibling—When teenagers lose a sibling, there are a multitude of emotions and feelings that can occur. There may be a sense of guilt over tensions and conflict that the survivor had with their sibling. There may be a new sense of responsibility if the sibling was older, but still at home. Teenagers may feel a shattering of the family unit, and have a new awareness of their own mortality. These characteristics are all in addition to the normal emotions of loss in losing a loved one. Leaders need to be sensitive to the situation of sibling loss for teenagers who may now be experiencing obsessing attention from their parents, or the opposite, that the parents are grieving so much over the loss of the sibling, that the surviving teen may feel overlooked and unimportant to the family.

Helping a Teen

- Anticipate that a teen's thoughts and feelings may fluctuate and sometimes be contradictory.
- As an adult, share honestly from your own experience with grief.
- Encourage peer support for the teen.
- It may be common for the teen's behavior to be defensive in covering up his or her grief.
- The teen may feel great responsibility for the death, regardless of the facts.
- Expect that some reckless behavior may occur as the teen acts out in response to grief.
- Allow for behavior that one minute may reject the parents and another may be childlike.
- Help to build a support team for the teen that includes understanding adults.
- Anticipate alternate patterns of extreme activity and also prolonged sleeping and inactivity.

THE UNIQUENESS OF DEATH BY SUICIDE

When a person completes suicide, it sends loved ones into a tailspin. So many complexities of the situation make this death most unique. It is most difficult to know how to relate to suicide survivors, but above all leaders must show that they care and give attention to them. Nonjudgmental listening is the rule, offering support to grievers who are dealing with stigmatism by society, and even friends and loved ones.

Here are some guidelines in helping a survivor during this most difficult season of grief. There may be a tendency to avoid encounters because of fear related to saying the wrong thing and the extreme awkwardness of the situation. Sharing one's deepest sympathy for the loss and offering condolences is extremely important. Based on the relationship a leader may have had with the deceased, sharing positive memories, relating experiences, simply providing a comforting presence are valuable ways of communicating empathy at a most difficult time.

One seeks to treat the death like any other death as much as possible. While there are differences, thinking about one's own losses and the ways in which people reached out during those times. All the emotions, sadness, difficult decisions will be there for them, and the leader may be able to assist in practical ways, or give a listening ear.

Averting terms like "committed suicide" is a more sensitive way to approach the death. More recently it is recommended by counselors to say "completed suicide" or "died by suicide." The word committed is often associated with a crime, and that is not the case with suicide.

As well, shy away from language that places blame on the person. Phrases like "they killed themselves," "ended their life" and "they took their life by their own choice" can contribute to the hurtfulness already felt.

Don't ask questions about the details of the death. Focus on listening, and let them share only what they feel comfortable sharing. There are specific groups that meet with suicide survivors, and it would be helpful to recommend such a group for those suffering from the overwhelming grief they are experiencing. For more helpful information, check out www.survivorsofsuicide.com.

CONCLUSION

When leaders are confronted with many different types of losses, it can be overwhelming. The best counsel perhaps is to be fully present in every situation. If one appears distracted or aloof or distant, it can send the wrong message to someone who is overcome with their loss. People want to know that you care, and that you identify with their loss. Every leader is different and personalities are different, but I would contend that if leaders feel emotion with someone, then they should not be embarrassed about that, but let it be expressed. The Bible tells us that Jesus wept when overcome with sympathy for Mary and Martha at the loss of their brother Lazarus. It is comforting to know that even Jesus empathized to the point of becoming emotional with those who grieved. It has often happened to me, and sometimes even during funerals. I don't apologize for that. It is who I am. If a leader is tenderhearted and becomes emotional in those moments, so be it. When people around us hurt, it makes us hurt, too. When people we love are grieving, it makes us grieve as well. The important issue is to be authentic in expressing love and concern in each situation. People will appreciate that you care, and that's what matters most.

PART III

COACHING OTHERS IN GRIEF

CHAPTER SEVEN

EDUCATING OTHERS TO
HELP THOSE WHO GRIEVE

Rejoice with those who rejoice; mourn with those who mourn.
—Romans 12:15, NIV

A most horrible thing happened in my family in 2005, but it seems like only yesterday. My nephew Jimmy died in a house fire. Or so we thought. Soon it became evident that he had not died accidentally, but had been tragically murdered. And the murderer was his wife, who was looking to cash in a $500,000 life insurance policy. She injected him with a paralyzing drug while he was asleep, and then set the house on fire to hide the evidence. But the scheme failed. The drug was isolated in his charred remains. The wife was convicted of first-degree murder and first degree arson and sentenced to life imprisonment. But, our family was left reeling—so many issues, so much emotion, so hard to bear. It all seemed so senseless.

Anger, disbelief, overwhelming grief came to us all, especially my brother Denny and his wife Ruth. Jimmy was their second son, and seemed to be doing well with his career, his faith, and his family. And now, all that was gone. He had left behind a young son and daughter who no longer had a father. He was robbed of his future. His dreams and aspirations were gone. This all came as such a shock. Death by homicide brings its own complexities to the grief process. My family experienced a tremendous ordeal throughout the long arduous journey of prosecution, trial, and sentencing—all which delayed much of the resolution that was needed. And still, even after all the due process of law transpired, the loss was and is hard to bear. It was such a heinous and totally incomprehensible crime. Jimmy was a Christian, and we are comforted by the fact that he is in heaven. But, the feelings of injustice and hurt continue to this day.

While there were many people who supported our family, there were quite a few insensitive comments made about the death and family members. It still smarts to this day. There should be a school for folks who don't know how to relate to grieving people. Still, my brother Denny shares his testimony of how God and faith have enabled him to forgive and bring the hope of Christ to others who are hurting. It is a tremendous witness that has emerged from a hopeless tragedy.

KNOW WHAT'S RIGHT AND WHAT'S WRONG

Many people are well-intentioned when they approach someone they know who has experienced the loss of a loved one, but they don't know how to help the person. Often, they say the wrong things. Leaders are in a position to help educate, give counsel, and correct persons who want to help family, friends, or acquaintances deal with their grief.

The sentiment is often expressed by a person "I'd love to help, but I just don't know what to say or do!" No doubt we can all identify with that statement. When someone we know, whether they be close friends, coworkers, or acquaintances, experience the death of someone they cared about, naturally our hearts go out to them. We have a longing to bring some measure of comfort and be there for them at a very difficult time. Yet we are never sure how to go about it. Questions swirl around in our minds, like "Should I bring up what has happened or just keep it at a superficial level?" "How do I handle it if they become emotional and start crying?" "Are there any words I could say that might help?" It all seems to be so awkward. One might conclude that it is best to let the person alone. But that could be the worst thing one could do.

Here are some of the best and worst examples of things that people say to a grieving person:

The Wrong Things to Say to Someone in Grief

1. You had her a long time, didn't you?
2. At least he lived to a ripe old age. Lots of folks die young.
3. Be thankful that she is in a better place.
4. It was God's will.
5. You should be happy. He's not in pain anymore.
6. Time heals all wounds.
7. Aren't you over him yet? It's time to move on.
8. You shouldn't feel that way.
9. When it's your time, it's your time.
10. There is a reason for everything.
11. God will never give you more than you can handle.
12. You're young enough to have another child.
13. God wanted her for his angel.
14. He should have taken care of himself.
15. It's probably for the best.
16. You have to be strong.
17. I know how you feel.
18. You can always remarry.
19. Don't cry. It will upset the others.
20. Try to stop crying. He wouldn't want you to cry.
21. Don't feel bad; at least you have other children.
22. Try to be positive and look for the good in the situation.
23. Everything will be all right.

Many of these statements are not malicious in themselves. Some may even be truthful. But, in the context of grief they can come across as shallow and insincere. You might think people know better, but they don't, as exhibited by someone who should have known better. A family counselor turned up at the visitation at the church just before the funeral. As a fellow church member, she wanted to come and pay her respects. The congregation and friends had come to say goodbye to a young man who died while playing basketball from a heart attack. The counselor stood in line with the rest of the mourners, and finally it came her turn to speak to the young widow. After a few words of sympathy, she remarked to the widow, "Oh, honey, you're young. You'll marry again." The widow was astonished at the insensitivity of this statement by a so-called professional. Not only was it insensitive, it was inappropriate and rude.

A leader can be proactive in helping people to express themselves appropriately to a grieving person. These things can be put in a sermon, a newsletter, a blog, or on a bulletin board. It is a great way to educate congregants about tactfulness and courtesy. The following statements will be received in a more receptive manner, for they communicate an honest sincerity that will minister to those who are grieving.

The Best Things to Say to Someone in Grief

1. I am so sorry for your loss.
2. Words cannot express how I feel.
3. Just know that I am here for you.
4. I am here to help in any way I can.
5. You are in my thoughts and prayers.
6. We will all miss Sue, she touched so many lives.
7. My favorite memory of your loved one is …
8. I don't understand what you are going through. But I do care.
9. (Not saying anything, but just a hug or arm around the shoulder.)
10. I am always just a phone call away.
11. I wish I had the right words to say. Just know I care.
12. I feel for you at this difficult time.
13. This must be very hard for you.
14. I care!

Remember, words are not the most important thing when it comes to offering care to a grieving person. A brief statement of sincere expression with your accompanying presence goes much further than one might imagine in bringing comfort that is needed. People who care should be affirmed regardless.

AN AFFIRMATION OF THOSE WHO CARE[1]

I believe in people who care.
Even more, I believe in what these generous people offer others.
They bring care giving down to essentials:
They offer not abstract ideas, but personal attention;
Not definitive answers, but reasonable assurance;
Not empty platitudes, but authentic hope.
I believe the work they do
Is both deceptively simple and unusually difficult.
For their task is to offer those who so need it something irreplaceable:
their own humanness.
They bestow a priceless gift:
themselves, and the best of themselves.
They approach the other holding out what they have to offer:
their sensitivity, their belief, their dedication.
They bring into the open what they choose not to hide:
their woundedness, their honesty, their compassion.
What these empathetic people do requires real courage,
for they do not know how they will be received,
or if they will be understood.
What they give requires great perseverance,
For healing is a time-consuming process,
And staying with others in their pain
Is an energy-draining experience.
But if these souls did not perform their roles in the way they do,
Then in a very real sense the Word would not be made flesh.
The love would not be made visible.
And the Hope would not be made genuine.
Yet because such committed caregivers are among us,
We know the world is not just a better place
But ours is a better time and we are a better people.
We know that because those who truly care show us,
Day after day after day.
—*James E. Miller*

---

1. James E. Miller, *How Can I Help?* (Fort Wayne, IN: Willowgreen Publishing, 2000), 2nd edition.

SET THE RIGHT EXAMPLE

People are always watching leaders, to see how they personally handle grief situations. They have a great opportunity to demonstrate sensitivity, compassion, and tact in the way that they relate to those who are grieving. Whether it is at the home of the family, or at the hospital, at the funeral home, or at church, one's behavior and demeanor goes a long way in communicating effectiveness in these situations.

This includes not only the initial days of grief, but also the aftermath, the difficult process of following-up with those who have lost loved ones. The demands of ministry take over quickly, and if one is not careful, those who are grieving are left to themselves after a brief period of frenzied attention from church staff and parishioners. This must not be. There must be a way to demonstrate a full-orbed approach to grief that helps to see grievers through the entire process of their journey. The pastor who demonstrates a continued concern and remembrance of a griever will teach by example that grief is not an event to "get over" but an extended journey where attention is merited from those who care.

EDUCATE CONGREGANTS IN PRACTICAL WAYS TO HELP A GRIEVING PERSON

The following suggestions are excellent for leaders to pass on to their congregants and others who want to help grieving persons.

1. Be present for them.

While folks may be concerned about what they do to assist others, the greatest way they can help is simply to be there. Though words sometimes fail, presence speaks volumes about one's desire to come alongside a friend or loved one who is grieving. Grieving persons may sometimes act like they don't want any help, but in truth, they are more than happy when a person will take the initiative and show up unannounced. The vast majority of people will welcome such gestures of concern and care.

I learned early on in my ministry that I didn't have to say clever things or give great spiritual insights when with a grieving person. My presence counted for a lot, and just being there in silent prayer with them was a great comfort at crucial times.

In the book of Job in the Old Testament, there is the account of Job's great tragedy in losing his children, his property, his livestock, and his health. This left him in a most depressed condition. In the second chapter of Job, Job's friends came to see him, and sat with him quietly for seven days. While that may not seem profound, their presence and willingness to listen to Job's laments was a ministry in itself.

2. Listen with compassion.

Knowing how to listen is so much more important than knowing what to say.

- **Give them permission to talk about their loss.** Many persons who are well-meaning avoid mentioning the person who died, but often times the grieving person wants to talk about their loved one. They don't want that person to be forgotten.

- **Let them express their feelings.** It is important for the grieving person to know it's okay for them to cry and show emotion. Don't try to correct the person or tell them they shouldn't feel that way. They don't need judgment or criticism, but acceptance and acknowledgement of their feelings. As far as conversation, a good rule to follow is to listen eighty percent of the time and talk twenty percent.

- **Listen with silence.** Perhaps the person may not feel like talking. Encourage persons who are visiting to simply sit there in silence and let their presence speak for itself. Eye contact, a tap on the shoulder, a reassuring hug, or squeezing the hand can all go a long way in making the person feel that one cares.

> Honest listening is one of the best medicines we can offer the dying and the bereaved.
> —Jean Cameron

- **Let them tell their story.** People who are grieving need to repeat the story over and over again, about how their loved one died. This is a most cathartic process for them. One's patience lets them know one is willing to listen time and time again.

> "There is no agony like bearing an untold story inside of you."
> —Maya Angelou

- **Don't demean the loss.** Different losses have different impacts on people. If someone has had a similar loss, then one might share that. But don't pretend to understand their loss, and don't try to minimize what their loss is compared to yours or anybody else's.

- **Speak with candor.** If grieving persons want to talk about their loved one, respond in a forthright manner. Don't avoid the subject, but probe gently to see if they want to talk about their loved one and things they did, things they said, things that happened, etc.

One widow I know has kept her husband's bomber jacket from World War II. She sometimes takes it out of the closet and puts it on just to feel his presence. She gets the sweetest expression on her face when she shares this story. People should resist the urge to tell someone to take off a wedding ring, sell a car, pack away pictures, give away clothes, or dismantle a room. The best way to approach the subject is to ask sensitive questions. What does that mean to them? Let them tell you about it. You may hear some incredible stories.

3. Don't treat the person differently.

When people are grieving, other people around them often consciously or unconsciously react to them in ways that don't seem natural. It may be an effort to protect them or not wanting to make them feel uncomfortable. Sometimes it is as if one may be walking on eggshells.

When individuals experiences the dramatic change that comes with grief, they struggle in many different areas. They can lose their sense of identity and feel like they no longer fit in with their friends. One of the most important things is to try to be natural around them. Don't treat them differently. If they enjoyed a good story or had certain interests in common, use that as a basis for discussion. This will help them to know that you consider them the same as before, even though in many ways they may feel everything but that.

4. Encourage the person to remember, not forget.

Part of the grieving process is the difficulty the survivors have in believing that the person is gone. Their ability to share about the person is efficacious to the healing they need. Reality settles in as they continue to talk about their loved one. Encouraging them to verbalize and remember many things about their loved helps them treasure memories and accept the death. In this way, they can put the death in perspective, remembering the past but also recognizing the need to take steps in rebuilding their life.

They often like to share humorous stories, places they have gone together, special events in the person's life, and pictures.

A woman in Wisconsin lost her only son in a Marine Corp helicopter crash. For years she could not escape the dark cloud of grief. She kept her son's room intact just as he had left it. Eventually, she began to notice how frequently helicopter crashes were reported on the news. She kept thinking of other families facing tragedies like her, and wondering whether she could do something to help. Now, whenever a military helicopter crashes, she sends a packet of letters and helpful materials to an officer in the Defense Department, who forwards the packet on to the affected family. About half of them strike up a regular correspondence, and in her retirement this Wisconsin woman directs her own "community of suffering." The activity has not solved the grief for her son, of course, but it has given her a sense of meaning, and she no longer feels helpless against that grief.

—Philip Yancey
The Jesus I Never Knew

5. Take the initiative with offers to help.

Many persons who are well-intentioned will say to someone who is grieving, "Call me if you need anything." While that gesture is certainly appreciated, it's so much greater to simply look for things that can be done and
do them! Grievers may not be aware of what is needed with the confusion
they feel. So, it is better to take the initiative and pitch in where needed.

    Here are some practical suggestions to help a grieving person:

- Mow the lawn if needed.
- Shop for groceries.
- Help with the wash.
- Help clean the house.
- Help watch the children.
- Help receiving phone calls and guests in their home.
- Take in food if needed.
- Help with forms or bills.
- Pick the children up from school.
- Take them to places they need to go.
- Go for a walk with them.
- Help with the pets.
- Take them to lunch.
- Share in an activity that they enjoy (puzzles, games, etc.).
- Go to a movie together.

6. Resist the urge to fix things for them.

As a friend or neighbor, one may have the desire to take over and help grieving persons do what you think they need to do, like get rid of their loved
one's clothes, clean out the closet, and bag up all their things. While the
desire may be noble, it is not your place to do this. You are putting yourself
in a position of judgment about what they need to do. Different people
take different amounts of time to deal with such matters. One lady let her
husband's stuff hang for two years. Another one left his chair in its place for
over a year. It takes time for persons to absorb the loss, and realize the need
to deal with these matters. Give them time. A gentle nudge may be okay,
but resist the temptation to fix everything how you think it should be. You

have to remember that for the griever, the things are no longer just things. They become special items that keep memories alive and allow the person to stay connected with loved ones.

7. Be aware of warning signs.

It is quite usual for grieving persons to feel that they are losing their minds, or going crazy. Many of their symptoms are normal for individuals who have lost a loved one. But as time goes on, there may be signs that people are experiencing complicated grief. You as a leader can be on the lookout and help others who are close to the person to keep a watch on him or her for anything that may indicate that grief has turned to deep depression.

The person should be encourage to seek professional help, especially if deep grieving symptoms prevail after a period like six months or so.

- Trouble functioning in everyday life.
- Obsessive focus on the death.
- Prevailing bitterness, anger, or guilt.
- Decline in personal hygiene.
- Dependency on alcohol or drugs.
- Inability to enjoy simple things in life.
- Confusion that continues long term.
- Withdrawing from others.
- Continuous feelings of hopelessness.
- Talking about dying or suicide.

It is wise to be tactful in expressing your views regarding the person's situation. If you do, utilize "I" statements that might say "I am concerned about your withdrawing from others. You seem to be more reclusive. How can I help?" As well, you might encourage the griever to seek professional help if the situation seems to warrant it.

8. Pay special attention to difficult days.

Grief is not an event that comes all at once. It is an extended process, and when special days like birthdays, anniversaries, vacations, and holidays come along, they can be extremely difficult for the grieving person. Other days like the anniversary of the person's death, Valentines' Day, or a special event that was shared, can reignite the full emotions of grief for a person. How can they be helped during these times? A card, a phone call, a brief visit, an invitation to coffee or lunch at those times can be most meaningful. Just being remembered at those times makes it special for grievers to know they're not forgotten.

IS THERE A CHRISTIAN SHORTCUT TO WORKING THROUGH GRIEF?

There is no doubt that a person of faith often copes better with grief than persons who have no active faith, at least in my experience as a pastor. Faith provides a solid resource to help individuals cope and benefit from the support that is provided through a community of faith. But sometimes Christians can be shortsighted about the traumatic effects of grief upon even the most dedicated believer. This can create a feeling of guilt among those who are grieving, who feel that they are not measuring up to expectations that are placed upon them in their church.

The following sentiments may be expressed by people of faith feeling those pangs of guilt:

- **Being a Christian means I will see my loved one again, so I don't need to grieve so badly.** It is indeed a great comfort to look forward in hope to that great reunion that will come with loved ones in heaven. But, regardless of your faith component, you still have the right and need to mourn your loved one. Your grief is not a weakness of faith, but a dose of reality that requires honesty and acceptance of your emotions.

- **I shouldn't feel so sad. I should feel joy for my loved one.** (They are not suffering anymore, and they are in a better place, they've gone on to be with our loved ones who precede them, etc.). While all this if true, the fact is that you are still missing them. Your feelings of sadness and despair at times is not unusual, even for a person of faith. It is a healthy response to loss, and necessary for you to work through your grief.

- **I have cause to celebrate that my loved one is in a new place where they are safe and free from the pains of this world.** Yes, that is true, there is cause for celebration in the fact that your loved one has graduated to the inheritance that has been prepared in heaven. But your authenticity in your longings for your loved one shows the level of your love and is a measure of honor and respect to his or her memory.

- **When I cry and mourn openly, I am showing a lack of faith.** No, you are not lacking in faith. You are demonstrating the quality of the relationship and your courage in expressing your emotions openly. Don't let people intimidate you or make you feel that you are lacking in faith. The truth is that they may be projecting their own immature faith on you with their judgment and unrealistic expectations.

Stay with Someone for the Journey

Grief takes time. A colleague of mine said, "Grief lasts as long as it lasts." For many persons, the process of healing is much longer rather than shorter. We must remember that when someone loses a loved one it is a most difficult experience in life to traverse. This side of heaven, you're not going to see that person again. That reality is quite stark and stinging. And what compounds the problem is that shortly after the funeral, many grieving persons feel abandoned, wondering if people really care.

A leader needs to help their staff, congregants, grief team, whomever, to know that grieving people need help beyond the funeral. People do care, but they tend to get on with their own lives, and are prone to neglect people who are still in the throes of their grief. So the support quickly dissipates and grievers often feel alone in their sadness and despair.

> The friend who can be silent with us in a moment of despair or confusion, who can stay with us in an hour of grief and bereavement, who can tolerate not knowing, not curing, not healing and face with us the reality of our powerlessness, that is the friend who cares.
> —Henri Nouwen, *Out of Solitude*

The fact is that we live in a culture that often seems to deny the reality of death. The experience of grievers is so contrary to what the culture tells them. And many grievers feel like they are failing because they are stuck in their grief. The erratic way in which grief is manifested in their lives calls for assistance in what can be a most unpredictable process.

People often say if you can get past the first year, then you will be better in grief. Certainly the first year includes many "firsts" that are tough—Christmas, first birthday, significant life events, all making grievers realize that they no longer can share those times with their loved one. That hurts, and it is miserable.

Grievers may not need someone every day, but they need people who will stay in touch, just to let them know they care and are thinking about them. If people are willing to pay the price, they can do a significant ministry to people grieving. Helping them work through by presence and thoughtfulness will go a long way toward helping them heal. Grieving individuals experience yearnings and have wishes for their lives and how they wished people would treat them and care for them.[2]

---

2. Cited by http://griefnet.org/library/prose/wishlist.html; accessed October 30, 2014.

CHAPTER EIGHT

IMPLEMENTING A GRIEF MINISTRY

*He comforts us in all our affliction, so that we may be able to
comfort those who are in any kind of affliction, through the
comfort we ourselves receive from God.*
—2 Corinthians 1:4, HCSB

Grief over the loss of a loved one can produce a tough emotional situation for an extended period of time. Who will stand in the gap and provide services and support during those crucial days when a person or family is reeling from loss? There is no better group to provide loving ministry than a congregational family. The way that a church reaches out to a family when a loved one dies makes a great impact on the survivors for the rest of their lives. I spoke at length with a friend who went through such a needful time, and asked how the church responded to his significant loss. This active church member shared some significant answers to

> A grieving person may have an overwhelming feeling that their grief is a prison sentence that must be endured for life.... A support system is necessary to provide tools to help a person grieve a loss in a healthy way. One way of providing this aid is by forming a bereavement ministry.
> —Angus Koolbreeze

questions that I posed related to the support given him and his family after losing his spouse.

How did your pastor respond to you and your family when you lost your spouse? "My spouse died after an extended illness that left her in a semi-vegetative state for four years in a nursing facility. Within twenty minutes of her death, I had called my pastor to let him know. We had been attending the church for eight years at that time, and I had taught an adult couples Sunday School class for several years. The pastor expressed his sympathies and offered to come to the nursing home, but I told him that the funeral director was already on the way and I would be leaving shortly. He didn't offer to come to the house, nor was there a personal visit before the funeral or after. A funeral service was held at the church three days later, and the church provided a luncheon following the service. Other than seeing him at church on Sundays, there was no other personal interaction following my wife's death until nine months later we had a brief conversation at a church event."

How did the church respond? "One family in the church responded the very same day by bringing over some food and in the weeks that followed, several families took turns providing a meal once a week (at that time I had two younger children still at home). Their desire to help seemed genuine and was greatly appreciated, although, in hindsight, I wish I had said 'no thank you.' After a few weeks, I felt somewhat awkward being quizzed by people about what to fix or not fix. If a church decides to provide such a ministry, I think it would have been better to have had one point person deal with the family. Due to my job, I frequently traveled, and one or two families were wonderfully helpful in providing care for my two younger ones while I was out of town. Without them, I wouldn't have been able to continue in that position."

What were you expecting in terms of help? "I really had no expectation of help since I had been a somewhat 'single' dad for more than eight years, caring for an invalid wife, two preschoolers, and three teens. My deepest need was not especially for physical help, although keeping up with meals, laundry, and cleaning was always a challenge (the last of those three usually got short shrift!). More than anything, I would have wished for some men that I knew in the church to come alongside and extend friendship and spend time with me. More than anything, I felt alone and isolated—a single man with no wife who didn't fit with couples yet wasn't a senior citizen. I did try to go to a couple of Sunday School class events but stopped after realizing that I was the odd duck. It was obvious that a church group built around couples didn't know how to accept a single parent (then at least). One dear brother did make an effort to reach out to me with lunch invitations, and I have always been grateful for that. I did struggle deeply with depression in the year that followed and ended up hospitalized with exhaustion from sleep deprivation and depression. It took another year to climb back slowly to a stronger emotional state. I'm not sure I ever felt during those long months that there were other men who cared deeply enough for me to make an effort to share in that struggle. That compounded the sense of loneliness and depression more than anything."

What counsel would you give to a pastor, based on your own experience? "I had been a pastor for thirteen years prior to changing careers. My guiding principles then were 'presence, listening, support.' A pastor can only truly express his love and concern by his presence in the crisis of grief. Not that families want a helicopter pastor hovering over them—but there needs to be an initial response, always in person if possible, to express support and address any issues with which he can be of assistance. (On numerous occasions I would present with the family at the time of death when an elderly person was involved). During that time, the pastor needs to listen with sensitivity to what is said. What *he* says is not so important as what *they* say. Where is this person at this given time? Is this person experiencing the shock of grief? Does this individual need very direct support? What family support structures exist? Are there spiritual issues that need to be addressed? Is there anger, towards others or God, that can be addressed at a later date? Can the pastor provide the safety net of compassion to let that person vent those feelings, without judgment? What physical needs can be addressed? Does this person need help with funeral planning? What financial resources are available? Finally, there is ongoing support, after the initial shock of loss and during the on-going grieving process. Regular monthly or every other month visits or phone calls should be made. The pastor should try to assess during this time what is happening with the person. Where is this individual in the grieving process? What appropriate support is needed? Is the person open to grief counseling services? Special sensitivity should be given to every special event that first year: the first holidays, the first birthday, the first anniversary for a married person, and the first anniversary of the loved one's death should be noted. A simple statement such as, 'I know this must be a difficult day for you without (name), and I want you to know that I'm praying for you' can mean the world to the grieving person."

How did you feel about the overall experience? "Six years later, I remarried a lovely woman who had lost her husband the year before my wife died. In comparing our experiences, we found that we both had been through many of the same emotions. There was the pain of loss compounded by the sense of being abandoned by 'friends' at church (we both attended similar churches in nearby towns). My wife felt especially hurt over comments that her now 'single' status made her a temptation to married men in the church! Both of us left the churches we had been a part of within a year or two. While time has lessened that hurt, for both of us there was still a good deal of hurt that we had to work through. Now, over ten years later, the pain of those rejections from others in the body of Christ has lessened, but the disappointment has not. For both of us, it's made us try harder to reach out to those we know who are working through the pain of grief and loss. We don't want them to experience what we went through."

WHAT'S A CHURCH TO DO?

From this testimonial it is obvious that churches can meet or miss important opportunities for ministry when a member or a person in the community dies. A system of support is essential to those who are working through their grief after losing a loved one. It is a fair assumption that one's church should be an important cog in the wheel of that support. The landscape of grief work has changed over the last twenty years. While there were few churches individually engaged in grief ministry then, in more recent times, many churches are individually becoming involved in offering grief ministry to their parishioners and to those outside the church as well. Initiating a grief ministry can lead to a significant outreach that will complement the other ministries within the church and the greater community.

Stating the Purpose

Up front it would be most helpful in establishing the nature of the ministry to grieving persons in practical terms, i.e. its purpose. One such statement could be: "The purpose of the grief benevolence ministry is to assist the pastor/staff in providing love, support, and practical assistance to those individuals in the congregation and community who have lost a loved one by death." Whatever the specifics of the statement, communicating clearly the purpose of the grief bereavement ministry is essential.

Making Preparation

Sometimes churches can launch new ministries without appropriate preparation and readiness for such ministry. Perhaps the place to begin is to gather like-minded persons together for the purpose of prayer and spiritual preparation. Seeking God's will and timing for such an important ministry is an absolute prerequisite. Familiarity with grief and understanding the grieving process is essential. Alan Wolfelt's book *Understanding Your Grief* would be an excellent tool to use with educating one's team about the grief process. The "ten touchstones" include virtually every aspect of the grief process from the impact of death until reconciliation with the loss and integrating it into one's life. No church should go willy-nilly into a grief ministry simply because it would be a great thing to do. Ask the right questions. Is it going to be a ministry only to those who have lost loved ones? Or, will it incorporate other losses, such as divorce, jobs, etc. Defining one's direction is important. For the purpose of this book, we will deal only with loss by death.

Doing One's Homework

Consult other professionals and grief counselors in the area. Find out what similar ministries and resources are offered in the community. Determine if there is a need for such a ministry in your church. There may be grief agencies already in existence that provide guidance and grief support groups for those individuals who have lost loved ones. They serve as an important link in grief ministry. It is not necessary to duplicate services that are already offered. But perhaps the local church can still engage in meaningful ministry that serves a valuable purpose in nurturing people toward hope and healing in their lives.

Devising a Plan

The Scope and Direction—It is important to ask questions that will help define the components of the ministry—What are the needs of the congregation? What are the needs that exist in the community? What are the goals for the ministry? Who will provide the leadership?

The Target Group—Will the church focus on widows and widowers? What about children? Parental loss? Will the group be devoted to one type of loss, or a mixture of losses? Most church groups seem to focus on mixed losses, but in my experience the most effective groups deal with a singular loss, such as the loss of a spouse, or loss of a child, etc.

Naming Your Ministry—Choose a name "New Beginnings," "Healing Hope," or another title that is easy to remember and has a positive ring that resonates with the goals of your ministry.

Promoting the Ministry—Utilizing bulletins, announcements, websites, facebook, other social media, radio public announcements, flyers, free publications—all will serve to get the word out. Of course, word of mouth often is the best means to communicate as individuals are helped through the ministry that you provide.

Forming a Team

Leadership—While the pastor does not need to necessarily lead the grief ministry, he or she needs to be involved in the planning process. Other than pastoral leadership, credentialed licensed personnel—if they are available to your congregation—can provide excellent counsel that will enhance the value of the ministry. There are many grieving people who feel like they are shipwrecked because of their loss. Through spiritual means, they may be directed toward finding faith and rebuilding their lives.

Members—Include people on the team who have a heart for people who have lost loved ones. It is preferable if they have experience with grief. But, the main requirement is that they want to reach out to others who are hurting.

Implementing a Grief Ministry

Perhaps it is best to take the position where the church is currently and move from there. My philosophy is to start small and grow strong. Taking too much of a chunk of implementation might be a formula for failure. Many churches are already engaged in providing a meal after the funeral, etc. Take that and build from there. Consider the different avenues you can go in offering services and ministry, and prioritize the steps that need to be taken. As a facet of ministry is added in each phase, the ministry will take on a significant role and people will begin to take note of the wonderful way they can reach hurting people throughout their grief journey. One important component may be the formation of a grief support group.

The church is in a unique position to bring people together who have recently lost loved ones. Persons may be invited to an initial gathering where they can be enlisted to participate in a grief support group. This group can help to normalize a person's grief, educate them regarding the grief cycle, provide a time for listening and sharing, in addition to prayer. A support group may meet weekly or monthly depending on the local needs and times available.

There are many considerations when you seek to initiate a grief support group. Who will lead the group? I think it is preferable to have qualified professionals to lead the grief support group. They have the skills, the experience, and the qualifications to handle many different situations. But still, many grief support groups are effectively peer-led by ministry volunteers across the country. It is not absolutely necessary to have the groups led by licensed clinicians. But understand that there are limitations, and also a church should consider the issue of liability. In the litigious society in which we live today, even churches are vulnerable to lawsuits when counsel or guidance is misconstrued or a person does physical harm to themselves. Thus, there is an advantage of having specially trained counselors to help facilitate the group is worthy of consideration.

Some Questions to Consider

- **What materials will you use for the group?**
- **How will the group be promoted?**
- **Should it be a mixed grief group or a singular grief group (spouse, parent, child, etc.)?** I have led both single loss and mixed groups. In my own church, I led a mixed group and it worked fairly well. There were mostly widows in the group, and by virtue of the unique loss, discussion seemed to be more relevant to their situation. But, all in all, it worked okay. Still, I think a spousal loss group, a parent-loss group, or a child-loss group works best if individuals have experienced the same type of loss. It binds the group together in a greater way because of the commonality among the participants.
- **How long will the group last?** I have led groups for different periods of time—sometimes eight weeks, sometimes ten or eleven weeks, depending on the need. I usually use the first meeting to do introductions, and allow participants to tell their story about

their loved one. An important document is a covenant which is presented to each individual. Confidentiality and respect for other participants is essential. Following is an example of the type of agreement to be signed by those in the group.

CONFIDENTIALITY AGREEMENT
Grief Support Group

This support group is sponsored by _____.
Meetings are intended to provide information about the grief process as well as provide the opportunity for sharing feelings with others who are in similar situations. This is not intended to be therapeutic intervention.

Commitments to yourself and the group:

Total Honesty
You can only complete the healing process if you are totally honest. However, there may be details of your life that you are unwilling to reveal to others. That is okay. All you need to do is tell the emotional truth about the event of experience. The focus on our group is on feelings, not the facts of a situation.

Confidentiality
This program has a commitment to Absolute Confidentiality. Anything of a personal nature that you hear in this program is and must be treated as confidential. The safety of this program and the safety of your individual growth and healing hinge upon adherence to the principle of confidentiality.

Uniqueness and Individuality
Every relationship is totally unique, each set of recovery communications is also unique. No one else's opinion is important other than the griever herself or himself. Again, the safety of this group and your individual growth and healing hinges on each person being able to communicate their own thoughts and feelings, without interruption, analysis, criticism, or judgment.

I have read and understand the information above and will keep those commitments:

Name:_____Date:_____

PROGRAM OPTIONS FOR GRIEF SUPPORT GROUPS

Following are some resources that may be used for training and programming related to grief benevolence ministry and grief support groups.

GRIEFSHARE

GriefShare is a lay-driven program from http://www.churchinitiative.org/that uses DVDs, workbooks, and small groups to facilitate a grief ministry. It advertises that it is "a Christ-centered grief recovery ministry." Many evangelical churches have used the Grief-Share program and found it an effective tool in helping grieving persons. It includes promotional resources and tools that will enhance its use. This program contains a strong evangelistic component. More information can be obtained at http://www.griefshare.org.

> We are spiritually best when we are shipwrecked on the island of God's sovereignty.
> —C. H. Spurgeon

STEPHEN MINISTRY

Stephen Ministers are specially trained lay members of our church who provide individual Christian care giving and support for people who are facing various crises in their lives, such as a terminal illness, grief, hospitalization, job crisis, spiritual crisis, separation or divorce, birth, adoption, or disability. These lay ministers receive fifty hours of intensive training through the Stephen Series. This is a confidential ministry in which those receiving care can be sure that their identity and disclosures will remain private. Stephen Ministers receive ongoing support and continuing education as they strive to provide the highest quality Christian caregiving. More information can be gotten at http://www.stephenministries.org.

LAY SERVANT MINISTRY

Lay Servant Ministries is a program of The United Methodist Church "to provide training opportunities and experiences to equip disciples of Jesus Christ to realize and respond to their personal call to ministry. Since each disciple is 'gifted' with one or more spiritual gifts (skills given by the Holy Spirit for the express purpose of serving the body of believers and thereby God), Lay

Servant Ministries strives to help disciples become aware of their particular gift or gifts by offering educational events to enhance and develop the skill level necessary for the full fruition of these gifts. It is an excellent vehicle for servant ministry skill development and has aided thousands of church members to be better servants of Jesus Christ, to become stronger church family leaders, and to more capably assist their pastors." See http://www.gbod.org/lead-your-church/lay-servant-ministries for more information.

Space does not allow the inclusion of all lay ministry training programs. Most denominations do provide some form of lay ministry training. It would be desirable to access specific information from those agencies for those who are interested in pursuing training related to their own theological persuasion.

IMPORTANT CONSIDERATIONS

What are specific ways that a benevolent grief ministry can meet the needs of grieving persons? A congregation may utilize existing groups in the church to help develop grief ministries: Sunday School classes can supply food, flowers, phone calls, visits and physical, tangible help. Pastor and staff can prepare for the funeral, graveside service, and counseling. Elders

When I was twenty-five years old, and very young in the faith, my youngest sibling, a wonderfully sweet brother, was killed instantly in an automobile accident. My family was unchurched and because my parents were unsaved, they were totally devastated and really unable to cope. The local church, probably thirty members at most, really rose to the challenge of loving my parents into the fold. Although very resistant to a Christian witness, my parents were very open to the care and concern that was shown by those dear people. God worked such a miracle out of that terrible tragedy. Many members of my family came to know the Lord. I thank God for the sweet witness of that tiny group of believers and for their willingness to give of themselves in a way that pointed this family to our dear Lord.

—Carolyn

and deacons can pray and visit the family. Senior adult organizations can fulfill some of the same roles as a Sunday School class but also can lead in organizing. Some of the practical needs to be met are as follows:

Ministry Action

Visitation—When someone dies, it is most difficult to know how to bring comfort to the surviving family and others close to them. Grief ministry includes a team who will regularly visit those persons who are grieving their loved ones. This effort will involve scheduling time to provide a ministry of presence to the grieving persons. It is not so much a matter of saying the right things, but simply being there to listen, to sit with them, to offer a prayer for their comfort and healing.

Cards—Members of the team can be responsible for sending cards and notes to those who are grieving. Words of encouragement, prayers that are offered, scripture verses, all bring comfort and blessing to those who need help at such a vulnerable time in their lives.

Meals—A great ministry to a grieving family is to provide meals during a period of time after the funeral. Some churches provide a meal for the family before or after the funeral at the church, or at the family home. Many times this occurs in conjunction with another committee or class in the church. But it is important for someone to coordinate this effort. As well, if meals are organized to be taken in afterward, someone should schedule and organize this effort. While everyone likes spaghetti and lasagna, the same meal can often appear if there is not care and consideration in this wonderful ministry.

Housekeeping—Coordinate volunteers to provide basic light housekeeping services for a few weeks. These services enable the grieving person or family to focus on their grief and make it through those tough early days without struggling over daily household tasks.

Phone Calls—It is essential to have skilled persons who are adept at making phone calls who will assist with arrangements. It is also importnat to have individuals who are gifted in empathetic conversation to call grievers, especially in later months when they may effectively inquire about their wellbeing, offering ministry, having a prayer with them, etc.

Coffee, Lunch—Meeting someone for coffee or taking someone out for a meal are most meaningful gestures and a form of ministry. One lady stated that after her husband died, the friends they had dined with after church on Sunday stopped inviting her to join them as she was now single. She finally took the situation in hand and invited herself to rejoin them. It is unfortunate that they didn't realize the devastating effect their exclusion had on someone who needed their care and inclusion. A social setting such as a restaurant can provide an atmosphere conducive to effective sharing and building a ministry relationship. A word of caution—It is important to exercise care in matching and not mixing genders for this type of ministry.

Intercessory Prayer—Do not underestimate the power of prayer. Bringing people together to pray for those who are bereaved is a most meaningful way to actively provide ministry to them. Sometimes, prayer is the last thing that is done. It should always be the first thing that is done, and should be recognized as a call to action as individuals are brought lovingly before God.

Faith Sharing—Persons may be led to experience a faith commitment as a result of a church's ministry to them. In the context of a grief support group or personal ministry and counsel, individuals may discover the eternal hope of salvation that comes through Jesus Christ. While a person's faith may not negate the emotions and difficult experience of the grief process, it will certainly provide healing and wholeness that will lead to fulfilling purpose and meaning in life.

IDEAS FOR GRIEF MINISTRY ACTION

The following tips for grief ministry action may initiate some creativity in approaching this valuable means of reaching out to those who have suffered loss.

- Cards and calls on special days—Father's Day, Mother's Day, Valentine's Day, Death anniversaries, Thanksgiving, etc.
- Provide a meal later on—three to six months after the death.
- Create a butterfly garden—where people can meditate and pray.
- Give a gift subscription or book to a survivor in lieu of flowers.
- Provide child care during the funeral visitation.
- Send a note or card on the anniversary date of the death.
- Enlist someone to house sit during the funeral.
- Secure some volunteers who will assist with Christmas tree and house decorations.
- Create a scholarship fund for surviving children in a family.

- Host a special memorial service or program for grieving families.
- Begin a mixed grief support group for different losses.
- Conduct an annual grief education seminar.
- Plant a remembrance garden with a plaque that lists the names of those being honored.
- Create a memorial scholarship to be awarded each year in honor of the person who died.
- Have a candle lighting ceremony on Memorial Day weekend to remember loved ones.
- Host a memorial walk to raise funds for support of the bereavement ministry or a special project.
- Start a bereavement library where books can be donated in memory of loved ones who have died.
- Match up grief buddies who can be active listeners and encouragers for grieving persons.
- Provide a sitter for a widowed parent who has small children and needs an evening out.

Susan was in a Sunday School class of eight-year-olds when her teacher, forgetting that Susan's sister had recently died asked the class to introduce themselves and tell something of their families. When Susan's turn came, she said, "I'm Susan Clark. I live with my mother and daddy. I have one sister. Her name is Carol."

"Oh," thought the teacher, "she's afraid to admit her sister is dead." But Susan continued, "My sister doesn't live with us anymore. Because she knew Jesus real good, she lives with him now in heaven, and because I know him, too. I'll be able to see her again one day."

As the children continued to share names and information, the full force of Susan's testimony struck the teacher—"Her name *is* Carol. Not *was* but *is*."

—Thomas B. Welch, Jr.

- Gather area grief support groups together for a networking luncheon.
- Create a resource directory of area grief support groups and counseling services.
- Enlist a team to provide stuffed animals to children who have lost a loved one.
- Sponsor a poster campaign in schools to bring safety awareness as a preventive measure.
- Host an annual grief retreat for the community with a special speaker and program.
- Comprise a scrapbook for grieving families with memory thoughts from friends and associates.
- Create a video with remembrances from family and friends for grieving persons.
- Schedule a prayer vigil for grieving families at a designated time.

Providing Grief Education

Ongoing grief education is an effective means of incorporating the grief benevolent ministry into the overall program of the church. The third and seventh chapters of this book are designed to assist leaders in providing valuable education to those persons who are wanting to help other grievers. There are often wrong notions about grief that comprise the fallacies about its scope and impact on survivors' lives. That is the mission of chapter three: to correct false ideas. The seventh chapter is written to help individuals know how best to reach out to their friends and relatives. Saying the right thing, doing what is practical to help, providing a presence that makes a difference—all are significant ways in which people can help others who are grieving.

CONCLUSION

The formation of a grief benevolence ministry is a serious commitment on the part of a congregation. But the inreach and outreach potential in helping those persons who have experienced loss can reap great benefits in the overall ministry of a church. Leaders would be wise to consider implementing such a ministry in order to extend the ministry to a significant number of individuals who may be overlooked in the church and surrounding community.

BEING A HARBINGER OF HOPE

"... and hope does not disappoint, because the love of God has been poured out within our hearts through the Holy Spirit who was given to us."
—Romans 5:5, NASB

I have many memories from my seminary days in Louisville, Kentucky. One memory that has stood out over the years is the funeral of a prominent local pastor who had died from a brain tumor. He was relatively young, and as a young seminarian I was struck with the solemnity of the occasion. The introductory prayer has remained with me all these years. It began: "God of our days, forgive us for our infantile expectations of life."

My initial reaction was that the prayer seemed to me a bit abrupt at the beginning of a funeral and struck me as odd. And yet, over the years, as I have reminisced about that unusual phrase, I have discovered that often we do have infantile expectations of life—even those of us who are leaders. We are real people and we are affected greatly by what happens to the people we love. And as we get caught up in the lives of people with whom we serve, what happens to them matters to us. When they hurt, we hurt. When they experience loss, we feel that loss as well. When they have profound questions, we have a profound desire to satisfy their queries. There are subtle pressures for us to provide answers, and if we're not careful, we can succumb to the temptation to play the role of God.

Many questions that people have about death and life resonate in our souls. From the perspective of faith, we hold certain truths about God and God's goodness that we seek to uphold. We clutch closely the hope that is steadfast and sure. But, in the precipitous and perhaps rare moments that our own doubts are exposed, we may feel some dismantling of the hero's garb that we desire to don as leaders. If we are honest, we admit that we don't have all the answers, and yes, some questions will not be answered this side of heaven.

Infantile expectations? Indeed, we can be naïve about our own expectations of God and the way that we think life should work out for those who honor God. But, along the way, we discover that what is necessary is to hold our convictions, and at the same time, give others the permission to find their way as we have found ours in faith. In time, the truths that we hold dear about eternal life and the destiny of those who love God will bear out. Meanwhile, we struggle sometimes with the mystery of life and the way that it unfolds around us.

We should take care of ourselves, and maintain disciplined balance in our stewardship of the ministry that has been given to us. The demands are always great, and the desire to be the best in what we do can sometimes cause us to compromise our other commitments. *A Necessary Grief* is not written to add to any leader's burdens, but to provide essential tools for effective ministry to those who grieve. Hopefully, your understanding of grief has been enhanced. Prayerfully, you are better equipped to help others in their grief journey. Expectantly, you will educate others who seek to help those who grieve. The challenge is great, but with preparation and commitment, you as a harbinger of hope will meet the tremendous opportunities for ministry that loss provides. With God's help, healing and wholeness will become a reality for those who are willing to do what is necessary.

PART IV

APPENDIXES

APPENDIX I

DIFFERENT AGES GRIEVE IN DIFFERENT WAYS

Adapted from the Dougy Center for Grieving Children[1]

BIRTH TO TWO: INFANT

Grief reactions:
- A baby is pre-verbal, sensory and physical in his/her reactions to loss. A baby may miss and ache for the sound, smell, sight, or fell of someone.
- A primary caregiver is a baby's greatest loss.
- A baby may express grief through general anxiety, thrashing, rocking, crying, sucking, biting, throwing, sleeplessness, sickliness, and indigestion.

How to help:
- A baby needs physical contact and reassurance for grieving.
- Include the baby in the process of mourning when possible and appropriate.
- A baby may be responding to an adult's grief.
- Patience will be needed through the hard times.
- Give the baby lots of holding and he/she will get through it.

---

1. Undated material from The Dougy Center, 3909 SE 52nd Avenue, Portland, OR 97286.

TWO TO FIVE: A YOUNG CHILD

Grief reactions:
- A young child will begin to examine death with words.
- A young child understands the profoundness of the event, but may not know that death means that the person is gone.
- A young child's primary expression of feeling will be through his/her play.
- A death affects a young child's sense of security.
- A young child can express strong feelings in his/her sleep and dreams.
- A young child may address a loss more spontaneously than an adult and thus may recover from it more quickly.

How to help:
- A young child will ask questions over and over; answer them over and over.
- Use simple and truthful answers.
- Include a young child in the dying and mourning process and rituals to help the child understand what has happened.
- Reflect and support a young child's reenactment of the death/crisis through his/her play.
- Have pillows to throw and hit for angry feelings.
- Maintain structures and routines.
- Tolerate the child's need to act younger for a while (i.e., regarding toilet training, sleeping with others, being held).
- Hold and love a young child during a nightmare and let him/her cry.
- Allow a young child his/her genuine joy and fun.

SIX TO TEN: SCHOOL-AGED CHILD

Grief reactions:
- Language is becoming a more important tool in the processing of a child's grief.
- Physical outlets.
- The family is a grieving child's main security.

- Peer relationships can help to support a child through a grieving time and to avoid feeling different.
- Grief for a school-aged child may affect school responsibilities.

How to help:
- Answer the questions and go into accurate detail if the child wants to know.
- A school-aged child may need some help with the confused thinking in regards to death (e.g., that death is not a punishment for bad behavior, the result of a monster that takes you away, the child's fault, or contagious).
- Offering books for the child to read alone or together can help.
- Art, music, dance, acting, sports, and active play are encouraged.
- Plenty of holding helps.
- Have intentional time to grieve together.
- Let the child choose how to be involved in the death and mourning process.
- Find peer support groups or help teach peer groups how to support their friends.
- Work with the schools to tailor the workload to the child.

TEN TO THIRTEEN: PRE-ADOLESCENT

Grief Reactions:
- The pre-adolescent is a young person full of changing behavior when grieving. Emotional turmoil is heightened by physical changes.
- The pre-adolescent may swing back and forth in dependence support from the family to peers.
- The pre-adolescent needs to engage in discussion that integrates significant events in his/her life; but physical outlets are still necessary.

How to help:
- Expect and accept emotional swings from acting childlike to acting like an adult.
- Expect internal body problems, headaches, and colds.

- Let the young person choose how to be involved with the family in the death and mourning process.
- Find peer group supports.
- Provide basic biological and chemical information about the death.

THIRTEEN TO NINETEEN: ADOLESCENT

Grief Reactions:
- Discussion about the critical events becomes the primary means of processing grief.
- Teens may become highly self-conscious about being different due to grief.
- Teens are self-centered and thus have an exaggerated sense of their own role in regards to death.
- Teens may fight their vulnerability in grief because it may cause them to feel more dependent on their family at a time when they are striving for independence.
- Teens are affected physically by the grieving process, especially in their sleeping and eating patterns.

How to help:
- Expect the thoughts and feelings of the teen to be contradictory and inconsistent.
- As adults, be honest in your own grieving and share in the discussions of the teen, when invited.
- Encourage peer support that may not include you.
- Expect that a critical event in a teen's life will stimulate the teen to ponder large issues, such as the meaning of life.
- Allow for their defensive behavior in covering up their grief if it is basically harmless to themselves or others.
- Expect that teens will feel unrealistically responsible for the death, significant to the deceased or vulnerable themselves to death.
- Expect that teens will express their anxiety over the death by being reckless with their own life to prove that they are not vulnerable.
- Expect that a teen may reject his/her parents one moment and appear childlike and in need another. Tolerate this inconsistency without accepting abuse.

- Encourage relationships with other supportive adults.
- Expects periods of high-energized activity or prolonged sleeping and inactivity.

Author's note: A Christian leader, in addition to being aware of the excellent secular material provided by the Dougy Center in dealing with age-specific grief reactions in children and teens, would apply faith applications where appropriate. In the author's experience, the involvement of the child in worship, study, and recreational activities within a faith community is a great outlet for the child's grief, whatever the age. Praying with the child, offering Christian guidance, answering faith-related questions, all are important components to the healing of the child or teen in their grief journey.

FUNERAL PLANNING CHECKLIST

Planning a funeral can be a complicated process, and quite overwhelming for grieving family members. Many of these arrangements can be made ahead of time, and that will lessen the burden on survivors. This checklist details most of the functions that are necessary at time of death.[1]

General Preparations
- Gather personal information for the obituary.
- Make a decision about flowers or a favorite charity to receive donations.
- Choose clothing for burial/jewelry/etc.
- Select a funeral home.

Funeral Home Services
- Choose traditional burial or cremation.
- If cremated, to be buried in a small container or placed in an urn.
- Select a casket or cremation urn/container.
- Choose the location for the service—funeral chapel, church, cemetery, etc.
- Choose visitation times—viewing or not.
- Select flowers—casket arrangement, other displays.
- Gather photos for display.

---

1. Adapted from http://grandviewparkcemetery.net/Funeral%20Planning%20Checklist.pdf.

- Decide whether there will be a bulletin for order of service.
- Service may be recorded if so desired.
- Choose memorial folders/acknowledgement cards.
- Plan service with officiant (music, hymns, solos, readings, eulogies).
- Select pallbearers.

Contacts to Make
- Doctor or coroner.
- Funeral director.
- Cemetery.
- Minister or church.
- Relatives and friends.
- Employers of family members who will be absent from work.
- Insurance agent(s) and financial institutions.
- Newspaper (obituary).
- Attorney, accountant and/or executor of the estate.
- City or county (death certificate).

Decisions to Consider
- Cremation or traditional burial.
- Casket (if traditional burial) or urn (if cremation).
- Cemetery property.
- Ceremony site.
- Music, singers or musicians; readings and/or prayers.
- Clothing.
- Flowers (inform mourners if they should send flowers or charitable donations).
- Pallbearers.
- Transportation to/from service.
- Food/facility for reception after the ceremony.

Other Considerations
- Write thank you cards.
- Preparing and signing necessary papers.
- Provide lodging for out-of-town guests.

Financial Considerations
- Doctor and hospital bills.
- Funeral service, including florist, music, and food.
- Cemetery property, including monument or marker.
- Cost of cremation (if applicable).
- Minister.
- Transportation.
- Newspaper obituary.
- Paperwork filing fees.

GRIEF AND THE SCRIPTURES

When You Are Afraid[1]

- The Lord is my light, Psalm 27.
- Lazarus is raised from the dead, John 11.
- Jesus arises from the dead, John 20.
- Jesus prays for his followers, John 17.

When You Are Worried

- Take no thought, Matthew 6:24–25.
- O give thanks unto the Lord, Psalm 107.
- Don't worry about anything, Philippians 4:6.
- Humble yourselves, 1 Peter 5:6–10.
- Be content, Hebrews 13:5.
- Do not fret, Psalm 37.

When You Are Bereft

- Jesus has compassion, Luke 7:11–15.
- Christ's victory over death, 1 Corinthians 15.
- Do not sorrow, 1 Thessalonians 4:13–18.
- Christ comforts, John 14:1–4.
- Jesus, the Bread of Life, John 6:44–51.
- Bring your pain to God, Isaiah 53:3–5; Hebrews 4:14–16.

---

1. Adapted from *Beyond Goodbye*, by Sherry Williams-White, New Leaf Resources.

When You Are Discouraged
- The Lord is my Shepherd, Psalm 23.
- Cast your burden upon the Lord, Job 11:13–19.
- Hear my prayer, O Lord, Psalm 102.
- Christ strengthens, Philippians 4:11–19.
- For this is the love of God, 1 John 5:3–11.
- The Beatitudes, Matthew 5:3–12.
- God watches over us all, Luke 12:6–7.
- Come unto me, Matthew 11:28–30.
- The Comforter, John 14:16–21; 26–27.
- The love of God, Romans 8:28, 35–39.

When You Need Comfort
- He saves the poor, Job 5:15–24.
- If you prepare your heart, Job 11:13–19.
- For in the time of trouble, Psalm 27:5.
- His favor lasts a lifetime, Psalm 30:5.
- Save me, O God, Psalm 54.
- The Lord is merciful, Psalm 119:50.
- In the day when I cried, Psalm 138:3–8.
- Comfort me on every side, Psalm 71:21.
- As one whom his mother, Isaiah 66:13.
- Be of good comfort, 2 Corinthians 13:11.
- The Lord has comforted, Isaiah 49:13.
- And even to your old age, Isaiah 46:4.
- They shall be comforted, Matthew 5:4.
- He that comforts you, Isaiah 51:12.
- I will not leave you, John 14:18.

When You Are in Trouble
- Preserve me, O God, Psalm 16.
- The Lord hears you, Psalm 20.
- In you, O Lord, Psalm 31.
- I sought the Lord, Psalm 34:4–22.
- A refuge in times of trouble, Psalm 9:9–10.
- I waited patiently, Psalm 40.
- I called upon the Lord, Psalm 118:5–9.

- I will lift up my eyes, Psalm 121.
- Yet man is born in trouble, Job 5:7–8.
- Be not far from me, Psalm 22:11.
- In the time of trouble, Psalm 27:5.
- I am in trouble, Psalm 31:9–14.
- You are my hiding place, Psalm 32:7.
- I cried unto God, Psalm 77.
- He shall call upon me, Psalm 91:15.
- Lord, be gracious, Isaiah 33:2.
- The Lord is good, Nahum 1:7.
- Neither be troubled, 1 Peter 3:14–16.
- My soul faints, Psalm 119:81–88.

When Friends Fail You
- Plead my cause, O Lord, Psalm 35.
- Yes, my familiar friend, Psalm 41:9–13.
- For it was not an enemy, Psalm 55:12–23.
- If your brother trespasses, Luke 17:3–4.
- Bless those who persecute you, Romans 12:14–21.
- Do you judge your brother, Romans 14:10–13.

When in Need of Peace
- Hear me when I call, Psalm 4.
- He will speak peace, Psalm 85:8.
- We have peace with God, Romans 5:1–5.
- The peace of God, Colossians 3:15.
- But we have this treasure, 2 Corinthians 4:7–18.
- God is our refuge, Psalm 46.
- O give thanks, Psalm 107.
- Peace I leave with you, John 14:27.
- The Lord will give you strength, Psalm 29:11.
- For the kingdom of God, Romans 14:17.
- And the peace of God, Philippians 4:7.

When in Need of Prayer
- Unto thee, O Lord, Psalm 25.
- As the deer pants, Psalm 42.

- David prays for mercy, Psalm 51.
- The Lord's prayer, Matthew 6:5–15.
- Pharisee and publican, Luke 18:10–14.
- Promise to disciples, John 14:13–14.
- Confidence in Jesus, 1 John 5:14–15.
- He shall hear my voice, Psalm 55:17.
- Cornelius' prayer answered, Acts 10.
- Ask, and it shall be given, Luke 11:9.
- By prayer and supplication, Philippians 4:6.
- Pray without ceasing, 1 Thessalonians, 5:17.
- I entreated your favor, Psalm 119:58.
- And you shall see me, Jeremiah 29:13.

When You Are Weary

- Eternal God is your refuge, Deuteronomy 33:27.
- Cast your burden, Psalm 55:22.
- Renew your strength, Isaiah 40:31.
- When my soul fainted, Jonah 2:7.
- Come unto me, Matthew 11:28–30.
- My heart fails, Psalm 73:26.
- Inward man is renewed, 2 Corinthians 4:16.

When You Need Patience

- We count them happy who endure, James 5:11.
- You have need of patience, Hebrews 10:36.
- Ask of God, James 1:3–5.
- Be patient, 1 Thessalonians 5:14.
- We shall reap, Galatians 6:9.
- Bring forth fruit, Luke 8:15.
- In your patience, Luke 21:19.
- The patient in spirit, Ecclesiastes 7:8.

When You Are Angry

- He that backbites, Psalm 15:1–3.
- Jonah's anger, Jonah 4.
- He that is soon angry, Proverbs 14:17.
- Make no friendship, Proverbs 22:24.

- An angry man, Proverbs 29:22.
- Be not hasty, Ecclesiastes 7:9.
- Whosoever is angry, Matthew 5:22.
- Be angry, and do not sin, Ephesians 4:26.
- Cease from anger, Psalm 37:8.
- He that is slow to anger, Proverbs 19:11.
- Put off all these, Colossians 3:8.

When You Feel That Justice Is Not Done

- Jonah is reproved, Jonah 4.
- Avenge not yourselves, Romans 12:19.
- God, to whom vengeance, Psalm 94:1.
- Justice and judgment, Psalm 89:14.
- The last shall be first, Matthew 19:27–30.
- Why do you stand far off, Psalm 10.

APPENDIX IV

INSPIRATIONAL QUOTES

If tears could build a stairway and memories a lane, I'd walk right up to heaven and bring you home again.
—Unknown

Let no one weep for me or celebrate my funeral with mourning, for I still live as I pass to and fro through the mouths of men.
—Quintus Ennius

If we have been pleased with life, we should not be displeased with death, since it comes from the hand of the same master.
—Michelangelo

Our care should not be to have lived long as to have lived enough.
—Seneca

Remember sadness is always temporary. This, too, shall pass.
—Chuck T. Falcon

He who has hope has everything.
—Arabian Proverb

Every person, all the events of your life
are there because you have drawn them there.
What you choose to do with them is up to you.
—Richard Bach

Perhaps they are not the stars,
but rather openings in heaven
where the love of our lost ones pours through
and shines down upon us to let us know they are happy.
—Eskimo legend

Say not in grief: "He is no more",
but live in thankfulness that he was.
—Hebrew Proverb

I do not want the peace which passeth understanding,
I want the understanding which bringeth peace.
—Helen Keller

A death is not the extinguishing of a light, but the putting out
of the lamp because the dawn has come.
Life is given to us, we earn it by giving it.
Let the dead have the immortality of fame,
but the living the immortality of love.
— Rabindranath Tagore

Life can only be understood backwards;
but it must be lived forwards.
—Sören Kierkegaard

Hope is like a bird that senses the dawn
and carefully starts to sing while it is still dark.
—Anonymous

Unless a man undertakes more than he possibly can do,
he will never do all that he can.
—Henry Drummond

Life's challenges are not supposed to paralyze you,
they're supposed to help you discover who you are.
—Bernice Johnson Reagon

Challenges make you discover things about yourself that you
never really knew. They're what make the instrument stretch—
what make you go beyond the norm.
—Anonymous

I look at life as a gift of God. Now that he wants it back,
I have no right to complain.
—Joyce Cary

When you were born, you cried and the world rejoiced.
Live your life so that when you die,
the world cries and you rejoice.
—Cherokee Expression

Whoever brought me here, will have to take me home.
—Rumi

Death—the last sleep? No, the final awakening.
—Walter Scott

Good men must die, but death cannot kill their names.
—Proverbs

It is good to die before one has done anything deserving death.
—Anaxandrides

I am ready to meet my Maker. Whether my Maker is prepared
for the great ordeal of meeting me is another matter.
—Winston Churchill

Do not seek death. Death will find you. But seek the road
which makes death a fulfillment.
—Dag Hammarskjöld

*We cannot banish dangers, but we can banish fears. We must
not demean life by standing in awe of death.*
—David Sarnoff

*The bitterest tears shed over graves are for words left unsaid
and deeds left undone.*
—Harriet Beecher Stowe

God's finger touched him, and he slept.
—Alfred Lord Tennyson

*Here is the test to find whether your mission
on earth is finished: If you're alive, it isn't.*
—Richard Bach

*Out, out, brief candle!
Life's but a walking shadow, a poor player
That struts and frets his hour upon the stage
And then is heard no more. It is a tale
Told by an idiot, full of sound and fury,
Signifying nothing.*
—William Shakespeare

*Lord, now lettest thou thy servant depart in peace,
according to thy word.*
—Luke 2:29, KJV

*For death begins with life's first breath,
and life begins at the touch of death.*
—John Oxenham

As men, we are all equal in the presence of death.
—Publilius Syrus

Death—the last voyage, the longest and the best.
—Thomas Wolfe

Nothing you can lose by dying is half as precious as the readiness to die, which is man's charter of nobility.
—George Santayana

There is but one freedom,
To put oneself right with death.
After that everything is possible.
I cannot force you to believe in God.
Believing in God amounts to coming to terms with death.
When you have accepted death,
the problem of God will be solved—and not the reverse.
—Albert Camus

Seeing death as the end of life is like seeing
the horizon as the end of the ocean.
—David Searls

Knowledge by suffering entereth, and life is perfected by death.
—Elizabeth Barrett Browning

If God hath made this world so fair,
Where sin and death abound,
How beautiful beyond compare
Will paradise be found!
—James Montgomery

Death came with friendly care;
The opening bud to heaven conveyed,
And bade it blossom there.
—Samuel Taylor Coleridge

There is no death! What seems so is transition;
This life of mortal breath
Is but a suburb of the life elysian,
Whose portal we call Death.
—Henry W. Longfellow

*Life is a great sunrise. I do not see why death
should not be an even greater one.*
—Vladimir Nobokov

*It is a far, far better thing that I do,
than anything I have ever done;
it is a far, far, better rest that I go to,
than I have ever known.*
—Charles Dickens

*I went to the woods because I wished to live deliberately,
to front only the essential facts of life,
and see if I could not learn what it had to teach,
and not, when I came to die, discover that I had not lived.*
—Henry David Thoreau

It is not length of life, but depth of life.
—Ralph Waldo Emerson

*Be not afraid of life. Believe that life is worth living
and your belief will help create the fact.*
—William Jones

*To touch the soul of another human
being is to walk on holy ground.*
—Stephen R. Covey

*The world is your mirror and your mind is a magnet.
What you perceive is in this world is largely
a reflection of your own attitudes and beliefs.
Life will give you what you attract with your thoughts think,
act and talk negatively and your world will be negative.
To reach a great height a person needs to have great depth.*
—Anonymous

And life is what we make it, always has been, always will be.
—Grandma Moses

It is one of the most beautiful compensations of this life that no
man can sincerely try to help another without helping himself.
—Ralph Waldo Emerson

The best and most beautiful things in the world cannot be
seen, not touched, but are felt in the heart.
—Helen Keller

Greatness and goodness are not means, but ends!
Hath he not always treasures, always friends,
The good great man? Three treasures—love and light,
And calm thoughts, regular as infants' breath;
And three firm friends, more sure than day and night
—Himself, his Maker, and the angel Death.
—Samuel Taylor Coleridge

That best portion of a good man's life,
His little, nameless, unremembered acts
Of kindness and of love.
—William Wordsworth

Our birth is but a sleep and a forgetting:
The soul that rises with us, our life's star,
Hath had elsewhere its setting,
And cometh from afar.
Not in entire forgetfulness,
And not in utter nakedness,
But trailing clouds of glory, do we come
From God, who is our home:
Heaven lies about us in our infancy.
—William Wordsworth

To laugh often and much;
to win the respect of intelligent people
and the affection of children;
to earn the appreciation of honest critics
and endure the betrayal of false friends;
to appreciate beauty; to find the best in others;
to leave the world a bit better
whether by a healthy child, a garden patch,
or a redeemed social condition;
to know even one life has breathed easier because
you have lived. This is to have succeeded.
—Ralph Waldo Emerson

If you learn from your suffering, and really come
to understand the lesson you were taught,
you might be able to help someone else who's now
in the phase you may have just completed.
Maybe that's what it's all about after all.
—Anonymous

Nothing is so strong as gentleness and nothing
is so gentle as real strength.
—Ralph W. Sockman

Expect trouble as an inevitable part of life and repeat to your-
self, the most comforting words of all: This, too, shall pass.
—Ann Landers

And God shall wipe all tears from their eyes;
and there shall be no more death,
neither sorry, nor crying, neither shall there be any more pain:
for the former things are passed away.
—Revelation 21:4, KJV

Honest listening is one of the best medicines
we can offer the dying and the bereaved.
—Jean Cameron

Character cannot be developed in ease and quiet.
Only through experiences of trial and suffering
can the soul be strengthened, vision cleared,
ambition inspired and success achieved.
—Helen Keller

Bear patiently, my heart, for you have suffered heavier things.
—Homer

I walked a mile with Pleasure.
She chattered all the way.
But left me none the wiser
For all she had to say.
I walked a mile with Sorrow
And ne'er a word said she;
But oh, the things I learned from her
When Sorrow walked with me!
—Robert Browning

They that sow in tears shall reap in joy.
—Psalm 126:5, KJV

The Lord God will wipe away tears from off all faces.
—Isaiah 25:8, KJV

Blessed are they that mourn: for they shall be comforted.
—Matthew 5:4, KJV

Although the world is full of suffering,
it is full also of the overcoming of it.
—Helen Keller

There is nothing the body suffers which the soul may not profit by.
—George Meredith

Trials give you strength, sorrows give understanding and wisdom.
—Chuck T. Falcon

Grief knits two hearts in closer bonds than happiness ever can;
and common sufferings are far stronger links than common joys.
—Alphonse de Lamartine

We must accept finite disappointment,
but never lose infinite hope.
—Martin Luther King, Jr.

BIBLIOGRAPHY

Attig, Thomas. *The Heart of Grief: Death and the Search for Lasting Love.* New York: Oxford University Press, 2000. The author's website is www.griefsheart.com.

Baggett, John F. *Finding the Good in Grief.* Grand Rapids: Kregel Publications, 2013.

Boss, Pauline. *Ambiguous Loss: Learning to Live with Unresolved Grief.* Cambridge, MA: Harvard University Press, 1999.

_____. *Loss, Trauma, and Resilience.* New York: Norton Publishing, 2006.

Bozarth, All Reneé. *A Journey through Grief: Gentle, Specific Help to Get You through the Most Difficult Stages of Grief.* Center City, MN: Hazelden Foundation, 1994.

Brown, Laura Krasny and Mark. *When Dinosaurs Die: A Guide to Understanding Death.* Boston: Little Brown & Co., 1996. (For children ages four through eight).

Byock, Ira. *Dying Well.* New York: The Berkeley Publishing Group, 1997.

Claypool, John. *Tracks of a Fellow Struggler: Living and Growing through Grief.* New York: Church Publishing, Inc., 2004.

Collins, Bonnie. "Expect Miracles," *Psychotherapy Networker*. Vol. 26, No. 5, Sept/Oct 2001, pp. 23–24.

Coniaris, Anthony M. *Daily Vitamins for Hurting Hearts*. Edina, MN: Light and Life Publ. Co., 1999.

_____. *Surviving the Loss of a Loved One*. Edina, MN: Light & Life Publ. Co., 1992.

Corey, Gerald. *Theory and Practice of Counseling and Psychotherapy*, 6th edition, Belmont, CA: Wadsworth, 2001.

Crenshaw, David A. *Bereavement: Counseling the Grieving throughout the Life Cycle*. Chestnut Ridge, NY: Crossroad Publ. Co., 1996.

Doka, Kenneth, ed. *Disenfranchised Grief: New Directions, Challenges, and Strategies for Practice*. Champaign, IL: Research Press, 2002.

_____. Second Annual Bereavement Conference, The Sage Colleges, Albany, NY, Oct 4, 2002.

Dyer, Wayne. *There's a Spiritual Solution to Every Problem*. New York: HarperCollins, 2001.

Figley, C., Bride, B., and Mazza, N. eds. *The Traumatology of Grieving*. Washington DC: Taylor and Francis, 1997.

Golden, Thomas. *Swallowed by a Snake: The Gift of the Masculine Side of Healing*. Gaithersburg, MD: Golden Healing Publications, 1996.

Gootman, Marilyn. *When a Friend Dies: A Book for Teens about Grieving & Healing*. Minneaplis, MN: Free Spirit Publishing Inc., 1994.

Greenberger, D. & Padesky, C.A. *Mind over Mood: Change How You Feel by Changing the Way You Think*. New York: The Guilford Press, 1995.

Hoy, William G. *Guiding People through Grief*. Dallas: Compass Press, 2007.

Ivey, A., et al. *Basic Attending Skills*, 3rd edition. Amherst, MA: Microtraining Associates, 1992.

Kauffman, J. ed. *Loss of the Assumptive World: A Theory of Traumatic Loss.* New York: Brunner-Routledge, 2002.

Kelley, P. *Companion to Grief.* New York: Simon & Schuster, 1997.

Kirkpatrick, Kate. *Praying through Grief.* Grand Rapids: Kregel Publications, 2010.

Klass, D., Silverman, P. and Nickman, S. eds. *Continuing Bonds: A New Understanding of Grief.* Washington DC: Taylor and Francis, 1996.

Kopp, R. & Sorenson, S. *When Someone You Love Is Dying.* Grand Rapids: Zondervan, 1985.

Kübler-Ross, E. and Kessler, D. *Life Lessons.* Scribner. NY. 2000.

Kübler-Ross, Elizabeth. *On Death and Dying.* New York: Scribner; first scribner trade paperback edition, 1997.

Kushner, Harold. *When Bad Things Happen to Good People.* New York: Avon Paperbacks, 2004.

LeShan, Eda. *Learning to Say Good-bye: When a Parent Dies.* New York: Avon, 1988.

Levang, E. & Ilse, S. *Remembering with Love: Messages of Hope for the First Year of Grieving and Beyond.* Minneapolis: Deaconess Press, 1992.

Mabry, Richard, *The Tender Scar: Life after the Death of a Spouse.* Grand Rapids: Kregel Publications, 2006 (2nd edition).

Manning, Doug. *The Funeral*, second edition, Oklahoma City, OK: In-Sight, 2010.

Martin, T. and Doka, K. *Men Don't Cry... Women Do: Transcending Gender Stereotypes of Grief.* Levittown, PA: Brunner/Mazel, 2000.

Miller, James E. *How Can I Help?: 12 Things to Do When Someone You Know Suffers a Loss.* Fort Wayne, IN: Willowgreen Publishing, 2000.

Mitchell, Kenneth R. and Herbert Anderson. *All Our Losses, All Our Griefs.* Louisville: Westminster John Knox Press, 1983.

Neeld, Elizabeth. *Seven Choices: Taking the Steps to a New Life after Losing Someone You Love.* New York: Delacorte, 1992.

Neimeyer, R. *Lessons of Loss.* Center for the Study of Loss and Transition, Memphis, TN, 2000.

Nouwen, Henri J. M. *Our Greatest Gift.* San Francisco: HarperOne, 2009.

_____. *Out of Solitude.* Notre Dame, IN: Ave Maria Press, 2004.

Nowinski, Joseph and Okun, Barbara. *Saying Goodbye: How Families Can Find Renewal through Loss.* New York: Berkley, 2011.

Oates, Wayne E. *Grief, Transition and Loss.* Minneapolis: Augsburg Fortress, 1997.

_____. *Your Particular Grief.* Philadelphia: Westminster Press, 1981.

Pread, A. D. *Transcending Loss: Understanding the Lifelong Impact of Grief and How to Make It Meaningful.* New York: Berkley, 1997.

Rando, Therese. *How to Go on Living When Someone You Love Dies.* New York: Bantam, 1991.

_____. *Treatment of Complicated Mourning.* Champaign, IL: Research Press, 1993.

Raphael, Beverly. *The Anatomy of Bereavement.* New York: Basic Books, 1983.

Rich, Phil. *The Healing Journey through Grief: Your Journal for Reflection and Recovery.* New York: John Wiley & Sons, 1998.

Schmemann, Alexander. *O Death, Where Is Thy Sting.* Crestwood, NY: St. Vladimir's Seminary Press, 2003.

Sanders, Catherine. *Grief—The Mourning After: Dealing with Adult Bereavement.* New York: John Wiley and Sons, Inc., 2001.

_____. *Surviving Grief … and Learning to Live Again.* New York: John Wiley and Sons, Inc., 1992.

Smith, Harold Ivan. *Death and Grief: Healing through Grief Support.* Minneapolis: Augsburg Fortress, 1995.

Staudacher, C. *Beyond Grief: A Guide for Recovering from the Death of a Loved One.* Oakland, CA: New Harbinger, 1987.

Welshons, J. *Awakening from Grief.* Little Falls, NJ: Open Heart Publications, 2002.

Williams, Robert A. *Journey through Grief.* Nashville: Thomas Nelson Publishers, 1991.

Winter, David. *Living through Loss.* London: Marshall, Morgan & Scott, 1982.

Wolfelt, Alan. *Understanding Grief: Helping Yourself Heal.* Muncie, IN: Accelerated Development, 1992.

_____. *The Journey through Grief.* Ft. Collins, CO: Companion Press, 1997.

Worden, J. William Worden, *Grief Counseling and Grief Therapy: A Handbook for the Mental Health Practitioner.* New York: Springer Publishing Co., 4th edition, 2009.

Zurheide, Jeffry. *When Faith Is Tested: Pastoral Responses to Suffering and Tragic Death.* Minneapolis: Augsburg Fortress, 1997.

GRIEF RESOURCE AGENCIES/WEBSITES

GRIEF AND BEREAVEMENT

New Leaf Resources

http://newleaf-resources.com
Website of Sherry Williams White, New Leaf Resources develops materials, community programs, seminars, and training programs. We have many new books, speakers, DVDs, CDs, even note cards to help people on their journey through grief.

Center for Loss and Life Transition

griefwords.com

GriefNet

http://rivendell.org
GriefNet is an online system that can connect you with a variety of resources related to death, dying, bereavement and major emotional and physical losses. It offers information and online discussion and support groups for bereaved persons and those working with the bereaved, both professional and lay persons.

Twinless Twins Support Group International

9311 Poplar Creek Place
Leo, IN 46765
219-627-5414

http://www.twinlesstwins.org
This international organization provides support for twins (and all multiple births) and their family members who are suffering from such a loss.

INFANT/PREGNANCY LOSS

A.M.E.N.D.
(Aiding a Mother and Father Experiencing Neonatal Death)
1559 Ville Rosa
Hazelwood, MO 63042
314-291-0892
This national organization offers support and encouragement to parents grieving the loss of their baby.

CLIMB
(Center for Loss in Multiple Birth)
PO Box 91377
Anchorage, AK 99509
907-222-5321
http://www.climb-support.org
CLIMB offers support by and for parents of twins, triplets, or other multiple-birth children who have experienced the death of one or more children during pregnancy, at birth, in infancy, or childhood. It provides contact listings, articles, and telephone and mail support to parents and friends suffering this kind of loss.

National SHARE Office
(Pregnancy and Infant Loss Support, Inc.)
St. Joseph Health Center
300 First Capitol Drive
St. Charles, MO 63301-2893
800-821-6819
636-947-6164
http://www.nationalshareoffice.com
This national organization serves those who are grieving the death of a baby through miscarriage, stillbirth, or newborn death by providing grief support information, education, and resources on the needs and rights of

bereaved parents and siblings. It sponsors more than one hundred local chapters nationally and internationally.

National Sudden Infant Death Syndrome Resource Center (NSRC)

2070 Chain Bridge Road, Suite 450
Vienna, VA 22182
703-821-8955 ext. 249
http://www.cdc.gov/sids
NSRC is an affiliate of the National Center for Education in Maternal and Child Health, which in turn is a service of the US Department of Health and Human Services. NSRC provides information, referrals, and assistance to parents and friends of SIDS victims, and distributes the Information Exchange newsletter. The center also provides free information sheets on SIDS.

Sudden Infant Death Syndrome Alliance

1314 Bedford Avenue, Suite 210
Baltimore, MD 21208
800-221-SIDS (7437) (24-hour hotline)
410-653-8226
http://www.sidsalliance.org
This national, nonprofit, voluntary health organization is dedicated to the support of SIDS families, education, and research. With help from more than fifty local affiliates, the alliance provides support groups, one-on-one contact, and strives to unite parents and friends of SIDS victims with medical, business, and civic groups concerned about the health of infants.

HELPFUL RESOURCES FOR COPING WITH GRIEF

Unite, Inc.

Jeanes Hospital
7600 Central Avenue
Philadelphia, PA 19111-2499
215-728-3777
This national organization provides grief support following the death of a baby, including miscarriage, ectopic pregnancy, stillbirth, and infant

death. It maintains local chapters and offers educational programs and information to those surviving these losses.

LOSS OF A CHILD

The Candlelighters Childhood Cancer Foundation (CCCF)

3910 Warner Street
Kensington, MD 20895
800-366-2223, 301-657-8401
http://www.candlelighters.org
This is an international, nonprofit organization whose mission is to educate, support, serve, and advocate for families of children of cancer, survivors of childhood cancer, and the professionals who care for them. This organization provides education, peer support, an information clearinghouse, referrals to local contacts, publications, and advocacy.

The Compassionate Friends

PO Box 3696
Oak Brook, IL 60522-3696
877-969-0010 (toll-free), 630-990-0010
http://www.compassionatefriends.org
A national nonprofit, self-help support organization that offers friendship and understanding to families who are grieving the death of a child of any age, from any cause.

MADD (Mothers Against Drunk Driving)

PO Box 541688
Dallas, TX 75354-1688
800-GET-MADD (438-6233)
http://www.madd.org
Mothers Against Drunk Driving is a nonprofit, grassroots organization with more than six hundred chapters nationwide. MADD is focused on finding effective solutions to drunk driving and underage drinking, while supporting those who have already experienced the pain of these senseless crimes.

The National Organization of Parents of Murdered Children (POMC)
100 East Eighth Street, B-41
Cincinnati, OH 45202
513-721-5683, 888-818-POMC (7662) (toll-free)
http://pomc.com
This national, nonprofit organization provides ongoing emotional support to parents and other survivors of murdered children. It will also help and assist victims dealing with the criminal justice system. Call or visit its Web page for support, information or to subscribe to its newsletter.

LOSS OF A PET

Pet Loss.com
http://www.petloss.com
This is a website for those grieving over the death of a pet or an ill pet. It offers personal support, advice, tribute pages, poetry, and more.

Pet Loss Partnership (PLP)
College of Veterinary Medicine
PO Box 647010
Washington State University
Pullman, WA 99164-7010
509-335-1303, TDD: 509-335-1179
The goal of PLP is to provide support for people grieving the loss of a pet. Call or visit its website to request a newsletter and/or other resource information.

SELF-HELP

American Self-Help Clearinghouse
100 E. Hanover Avenue, Suite 202
Cedar Knolls, NJ 07927-2020
973-326-6789
http://www.mentalhealth.net/selfhelp

This national organization provides information on local self-help group clearinghouses worldwide, which can help you find and form bereavement self-help groups. The American Self-Help Clearinghouse also provides free consultation on starting new self-help groups.

National Self-Help Clearinghouse
CUNY, Graduate School and University Center
365 Fifth Avenue, Suite 3300
New York, NY 10016
212-817-1822
http://www.selfhelpweb.org
This nonprofit, national service refers individuals to self-help support groups all over the United States. It will help you locate a support group in your area or refer you to a clearinghouse that will help you locate one.

American Association of Suicidology
5221 Wisconsin Ave NW
Washington DC 20015
www.suicidology.com

Bereaved Parents of the USA
P O Box 95
Park Forest, IL 60466
www.bereavedparentsusa.org

The Candlelighters
American Childhood Cancer Organization
National Office
P O Box 498
Kensington, MD 20895-0498
www.candlelighters.org

Concerns of Police Survivors (COPS)
846 Old South 5
Camdenton, MO 65020
www.nationalcops.org

Life Event Management~sm~ Services

http://www.lifecare.com
Helping Other Cope with Grief, 2001 LifeCare®, Inc.
http://www.foh.dhhs.gov/NYCU/copingtips.pdf

National Catholic Ministry to the Bereaved

P O Box 16353
St. Louis, MO 63125-0353
www.griefwork.org

National SIDS Resource Center

2115 Wisconsin Ave, NW, Suite 601
Washington DC 20007
www.sidscenter.org

NOVA (National Organization for Victim Assistance)

510 King Street, Suite 424
Alexandria, VA 22314
www.try-nova.org

National Organization of Parents of Murdered Children (POMC)

100 East Eighth Street, Suite B-41
Cincinnati, OH 45202
www.pomc.com

SHARE (Pregnancy and Infant Loss Support, Inc.)

The National Office
402 Jackson Street
St. Charles, MO 53301
www.nationalshare.org

THEOS (They Help Each Other Spiritually)

The Theos Foundation
International Office, 322 Boulevard of Allies, Suite 105
Pittsburgh, PA 15222-1919

Tragedy Assistance Program for Survivors (Taps)
1771 F Street, NW
Washington DC 20006
www.taps.org

Widowed Persons Service (WPS)

American of Retired Persons (AARP)
601 E Street NW
Washington DC 20048
www.aarp.org